The Marrakech Express

THE MARRAKECH EXPRESS

A Train
of
Thought

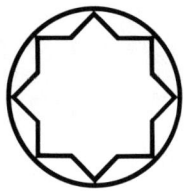

by
David Saltman
photos
by
Paul Hyman

New York  London

PS
3569
A2M3

Copyright © 1973 by David Saltman
All rights reserved
including the right of reproduction
in whole or in part in any form
Published by Links Books
33 West 60 Street, New York 10023 and
78 Newman Street, London W.1

First printing
Standard Book Number: 0-8256-3006-1
Library of Congress Catalog Card Number: 72-94091
Printed in the United States of America

Designed by Uli

CONTENTS

I		1
II	Socko! Morocco!	17
III	Marrakech: Certificate "X"	35
IV	In Which We Consult the Myths of Free Men	85
V	Lessons: For the Body, for the Mind, for the Soul, for the Spirit	127
VI	Whole Earth Liberation Front	155

Appendix

    1. A Magic Lesson   162

    2. A Music Lesson   168

    3. An Arabic Lesson   175

I CHING
   Hêng.
   DURATION. Success. No blame.
   Perseverance furthers.
   It furthers one to have somewhere to go.

                        Change:
INNOCENT BEHAVIOR BRINGS GOOD FORTUNE.
Thunder and wind: the image of DURATION.
Thus the superior man stands firm and does not
    change his direction.

I

Ocean voyage. Fifth day.
　　　Phantom ship of the Atlantic, flying proud rainbow. All abuzz with head trippery. Welcome to the travel agent special: New York to Tangier on Yugoslav freighters. $180 one way for a nine-day trip. Just the ticket for winterbound Americans contemplating the occult, peace and quiet, or a piece of the action.
　　　For these were mind-boggling times in the Old Country. Madmen wielding ticklish electronic featherdusters had invaded the air and water. They were mostly reps for Fire and Earth, Advertising Partners. Many of us nomads were down on our backs with laughter, gasping for breath. The ones that squirmed out ran like hell for travel bureaus, and of course New York City was a major rendezvous since we were inconspicuous there.
　　　Modern nomadics--the art of getting somewhere. "Chef Kybernetes is out sharpening the contradictions," wrote a friend from Algiers. That about sums it up. Us longhairs were <u>splitting</u>, man, and that was it! Emigrés from Babylon. It was time to love it or leave it. We could counterattack later on through the soft underbelly, but the time was wrong just now. Just now, surplus value was filling a lot of freaks full of buckshot! The superior man keeps the inferior man at a distance.

Did you ever hear the story about the fisherman?
He caught fish after fish, stuffing his craw. When he quit, he was still hungry. Not from real need, just from his tongue's memory of good taste. He looked around on the beach and saw a sandwich, wrapped in a Baggie.
"Aha!" he exclaimed, picking it up.
"Oho!" he gloated, putting it into his mouth.
As he bit down, the sandwich and the fisherman began to jerk toward the river. A thin nylon line surrendered its camouflage, drawing taut. It came from the river somewhere.
--Derived from a line in a Bob Dylan song

Personally, we had postponed pet notions (like taking over a radio station) for some time and tide. The way we see it, the business cycle is heading for a showdown with the sunspot cycle. Us somewhat innocent bystanders had laid down our bets and now were skedaddlin' until the smoke cleared.

During this journey we meet a lot of people: all castes, all colors, all loyalties, all haircuts. The one clear light interpenetrating their dark lines is America. America the raped and raping, America the creative and destructive, America the fascist and revolutionary.

Let me put it this way. "Conditions are such that the hostile forces favored by the time are advancing. In this case retreat is the right course, and it is through retreat that success is achieved. But success consists in being able to carry out the retreat correctly. Retreat is not to be confused with flight."

That's straight from the big yellow book, as reprinted in the Whole Earth Catalog.

Zoom into my pal Bob and me leaning over the poop rail, discussing pirates and such.

"The earth is three-fourths water," I exclaim, squinting into the sun.

"And the pirates three-fourths salt," Bob replies. "A

spoonful of curry powder and a curl of opium, the rascally Lascars!"

"Alchemists of the forces of reaction!"
"Ancestors of American Express agents!"
"See-all, hear-all, know-all righteous nobles,
Students of commodities,
Sailors of the seven seas,
Purveyors of the certain and probable."

    It's true. But the Great Pirates found a microtome at the base of their spines when some scientists decided to muscle in on waters that couldn't be charted without a certain scope.
    Bob answers, "Hey, did you ever see this film about these people on a freighter?"
    Yeah, it's just like in the movies. Except more so. You get hot showers, wine with your meals, a dirt-cheap bar, Yugoslav mandolin by moonlight, and intricately involved with your brethren. You're all on a <u>freighter</u> to <u>Africa</u> together, for God's sake! Splitting the <u>feudal kingdom</u>.
    The other passengers ranged from Omega to Arcturus, all with an interest in international affairs. We're meeting at the Fertile Crescent for a reunion on May 15.
    Adjust the monocle. Clear the throat. Ahem--I quote from my notebook:

Thirty two (48) passengers without a plan, nary a payroll to meet (unless on the street in Tangier), new cash crop of splittee from thuggee, Sabbatical grace, 1970.

Dope dealers, dome builders, filmmakers, sorcerers' apprentices. Hash smokers, card players, Old Princetonians, party girls, backpackers, heiresses, UN interpreters, childhood friends of Ché, drum majors, deputy harbormasters, seventh-grade math teachers, and at least two genuine enigmas.

Splitting on the draft. Splitting with the bug-to-split. Splitting to meet someone, or to elude someone else. Splitting on an heirloom, on a hex, on a whim or a whammy.

"I just want to see Israel before I die," the UN interpreter told me. "I've already seen Cuba."

"Well, first we're going to Norway to buy a boat, then we'll sail to Sumatra where I'll try to get a gig doing photos for UPI, so then we can . . ."

"Just let it flow naturally, man. We can't make any plans." They ended up on a houseboat in Amsterdam, teaching music.

"Say, does anyone know this game 'baccarat' they play at Monte Carlo? . . ."

"I knew these people who went to Morocco last year and had the craftsmen make them a fucking table out of the shit, and they slid past Customs without even a blink!"

"I can't tell you anything, man. I've been planning this one for four years!" A girl sweet as a dewdrop.

"When it comes right down to it, I'd fight for the police! Even though some of my best friends are revolutionaries!" Stay away from that one. He was a dog breeder and he called the Yugoslav steward, named "Dinko," Dingo!

The long-haired "freak": "I used to be president of a multimillion dollar corporation in Boston!"

The nondescript "straight": "Yeah, man, when I was in Tierra del Fuego. . . ."

"It's fucked in America, man!" exclaimed Timmie, a New York girl from Berkeley. "Everybody's living on the fucking brink!"

"Do you realize if you took over all the television and radio networks you'd control the whole country?" rapped Sweet William, a gentleman from the South. "But personally, I'll just sip this mint julep. . . ."

"Man, all I want to do is go to Persia and lose myself in the eleventh century," said Ken, a quiet, reflective Bay Area artist.

Timmie added: "You know, I heard about these islands in the Indian Ocean where they got this huge treasure, some pirate . . ."

"That's not the Andaman Islands, is it?" asked Russ, a ski freak from Denver. "Why, I heard they got this dope there. . . ."

"States is fucked, man," Will says to me one day. "Fucking nowhere!"

"Yeah, I agree."

"Gonna travel all across India with the goats and chickens, on the third-class train," he continues. "Y'can get all the way across India for sixty bucks, man. Sixty fucking bucks!"

"Wow! That's far out!"

"Then I'm heading for Singapore."

"Singapore?" This is a new one on me. Most freaks going out that way end up in Bali.

"Yeah, man. I might have been accepted at the university there!" he announces. "And you know where I'm going after I been everywhere else in the world?"

"Where?"

"California!"

Talked out for now. Time to consort with albatross. This is the ocean, by God, and whoever doesn't give it proper respect damn well deserves his executive jet lag! The floor of the sky is three-fourths water, and so is the human body.

We know about politics out here on the ocean. It's not enough. Not subtle enough to counterpoise the forces we are dealing with. Not sinewy enough to resist chewing and sucking pests: not organically grown. Contemplating our ocean we know a great truth: for all the talk and fire, for all the bombings, Panthers, invective, left-right magazines, "heavy shit," and good intentions--politics is not <u>The Source</u>.

Take an ocean voyage and let <u>your thoughts</u> reflect on the black water. (Mind you, the oil squeezed from the Standard New Jersey pimple was licking at our wet suits! But the flying fish we questioned about it demurred they had schools to attend.)

We are after The Source. Political systems rise and fall, banks and merchant marines come and go, the pirates give way to Pfizer and American Express--Karl Marx and the Inca notwithstanding. Relative freedom is relative slavery.

Skyocean at night. Stars thick as a Christmas pudding. There's more things on heaven and earth than are dreamed of in the CBS newsroom. After all, how many puppet governments can dance on the point of a bayonet? How many space shots will it take to go nowhere? Was the black shitcloud over New York just done with wires and carny mirrors? Youth Wants to Know!

So now we're listing this way and that, trying to keep our sex lives trained on the horizon, our thumb prints out of the FBI Navigation Room, and our bilge pumped and primed for smooth reentry into Moroccan waters. We plan to ask those aforementioned questions to some shrewd Arabian tricksters.

I mean, we've just read a couple of National Geographics and talked to a few people, you know. Who knows? But we, my wife Barbara and I, we decided to take the plunge. And here we are, out on the ocean, slowly buzzing along toward Morocco. Haven't seen a <u>single other thing</u> for days. Repeat until you get it by heart: most of the earth is water, most of the earth is water. . . . Saline reconditioning shampoo. Rub it in real well, massage your overloaded scalp, rinse and repeat.

To break our heads in, we took a visit up to the bridge to learn about navigation. Met a fine Yugoslav fellow, named Mate, who pointed out that sailors don't have to wear watches. We told him hippies don't either. Mate's voice sank to a whisper and he hissed a secret into our fuzzy ears: "If you're on the Pacific, the sun rises in the Occident and sets in the Orient!"

Teeth chattering, we went below.

It's psychic economics. In the States our brains were honed to a frazzle. It got so we couldn't even see headlights in the rearview mirror without freaking and consulting McLuhan.

"Aw, it's just Berkeley," we'd rationalize, as we made our way through the checkpoints. But I remembered Berlin, and Mexico City, and Jerusalem, and a thousand others. This was IT, the real thing, no bullshitting around, Fascism with a capital Fat Pig.

We hurried home to catch the tailend of the news, something about shooting clubs in Dearborn. Followed by Truth Or Consequences. If Nixon had only asked that riddle about snake oil. Instead, according to old transcripts, he asked, "What's a Paradox?" Something buzzed, he leered and said, "Two Doctors!" and signed some Consequence Warrants. "Ughhh!" from the audience, but rules is rules.

It took a few murders to convince us. People's Park in Berkeley. Handwriting on the street, plain as the blood of a slain brother. News of Kent State reached us only after we were tucked safely away in the Rif Mountains in Morocco. "The hostile forces favored by the time are advancing."

The <u>I Ching</u> says the time of retreat is great. So Barbara and I bought a ticket on the first winter freighter to Africa. We had done active duty too long. North Africa seemed as good a place as any to lay out. You get a good class of people there: Cleaver, Leary, Ben Barka, the Queen of Ifriqiya.

We stocked up on grainy old flicks about the International

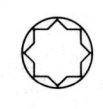

Zone, where the heroine ends up crawling out of the desert with her dress torn and tears caked on her face. Barbara got into veils and intricate lettering. We memorized "Casablanca." Consulted every available piece of travel literature, glorying in the thought of palm trees in January. Even made a stab at learning Arabic from a book--a bust. Learned to throw a <u>kris</u> and eat <u>couscous</u> with my fingers. We'd be ready for them A-rabs, <u>by God</u>!

The dentist warned us not to let them pull our teeth. Solicitous friends warned us not to let them know we're Jewish ("Aren't you worried?"). Everyone warned us not to drink the water, not to eat the food, not to talk to strangers, not to be conspicuous ("They hate Americans!"), and above all not to get involved in that DOPE SCENE!!

We took it all with a grain of salt. We were having too much fun consulting the freighter timetables. ("Let's see, if we go to Dakar and then Casablanca . . . or maybe the Canaries, through the Dardanelles and up to Odessa . . . there's a freighter every two months to Dar es-Salaam, then we can catch the mail boat from Durban to Bombay and stop at the Seychelles on the way!")

No doubt at all--freighter travel is HIGHLY DESIRABLE!!

Guaranteed friendships. No jet lag, no airport taxes, no thumbscrews upon embarkation. Maybe a wobbly gait for a couple of days, that's all.

And the crew is generally outasight! The doctor on our ship played mandolin and freely dispensed all drugs, advising a hit of slivovitz to wash them down. "I am not a revolutionist," he would say sadly.

So here we were, The People, on a throbbing Yugo freighter heading for the mysterious East, or Africa, or the Mediterranean, however you like it. The ocean breeze blew cobwebs off our pineals, and a few even began to swagger, ordering: "Keelhaul the bosun! Jettison the mizzenmast! Avant, ye swabbies, and luff to larbord!" It was High Fun and important work.

Ahh, yes. We were leaving Nixons and Agnews behind, where they belong, taking that heavy electromagnetic load off our skulls. A rich supply of blood was rushing to the dent it had left. We were OUT, by God, they don't ask your Social Security number on the high seas.

The psychic pulse went up to maybe a million!

"Shit, man, I'm gonna hitch across Algeria and Tunisia and then see them Pyramids. I don't give a fuck about the war. . . ."

"I heard they got these nomads out in Sudan, smoke this black hash. . . ."

"Dig it, man! When I was in Berkeley I met this cat. He took me over to see his cousin or something, and they lay this story on me about this chick in Egypt, man, she's the latest incarnation of Nefertiti! No shit! I got her name and everything. I figure if enough of us are hip to it we go to Cairo, see, and get a flatboat that we can sail down the Nile. . . ."

A nine days' wonder. We had been harrowed and fertilized, brushed and currycombed. Shaken well (from twenty-five degrees port to twenty-five degrees starbord). Prepare to eject, island-continent ahead, anchored to the center of time. As the seedling falls so sprouts the sprig. Gimme another slivovitz, shit, this is the last fucking night, ain't it, what the fug? Talktalktalk. O, crikey! My head!

Step outside to clear it. Party rages on in the ship's lounge, phantom freighter, Flying Dutchman, just stand out here in the cool salt spray get myself together. . . . Incredible sky. Punctures on a black diaphragm up the cosmic cunt. BUT NO! PROOF! A METEOR, A RED JETSTREAM, EXPLODING TO THE RIGHT!! CALL THE OMENOLOGISTS! LOOK OUT FOR INCENDIARY ACTION IN AFRICA SOON! JESUS, MOTHER OF GOD!!

"Hey, hey! I just saw a fucking meteor, no shit, a fucking honest-to-God meteor! Flying to the right! Blew my fucking mind out!!" A wondering chorus of "Far out!"

Suddenly the music stops and everyone looks toward the doorway. A sharp-faced man with shades walks in slowly, surveying the crowd.

"Good evening," he says casually. "Do not be alarmed. I'm just soliciting for the Dolphins' admission to the UN!"

II

SOCKO! MOROCCO!

                O, Tangier! Hash butcher to the World!
                City of the Skinny Waist and Separate Pads!
                Your green mountains can't conceal
                What your white houses hustle to reveal.
                For this is the mighty Maghreb!
                Lord of the West,
                Who fought off the invading Parthians,
                Who skonked the marauding Sassanians,
                Who beat back the heathen Turks--
                Only to be flummoxed
                By a certain Don Fulano de Tal
                And his ragtag band of American advisers.

If Algiers is the socialist maraschino on the peoples' pudding,
Tangier is the bottom of the bowl.

Bright the next morning, just off the boat, when who should fall in alongside but fifteen-year-old Mohammed, quick as a cobra lick, dark as brown clay.

"What hotel you go to?" he hissed.

"Istanbul," we answered, remembering the advice of a friend of a friend. "Or maybe the Royale?"

"Ahh, no! No! I take you to nice hotel, hot showers, very nice, you know--and then maybe we smoke hashish, eh?" Mohammed said slyly.

"JESUS CHRIST MAN! WE'RE JUST OFF THE FUCKING BOAT!! FOR CHRIST'S SAKE!!" I screamed, but it doesn't faze Mohammed.

"You from California? New York? California?" he asked with a shifty eye.

"California," I answered resignedly. "Here's all my money. Just leave my underpants."

"Hey, man, you ver-r-y clever," he said with a grin. "You want buy some kif? One gram, one dirham, cheap price," he chattered.

We were walking along the quay, passing little knots of robed Arabs getting loaded. They smoke from these long pipes with little bowls, just taking one drag and dumping the unburnt kif out by blowing sharply through the pipe.

Kif? Moroccan weed. Not to be confused with your Mexican grass or Middle Eastern hashish. Personally, I wouldn't buy any, though it makes a nice kicker to a pipe of hash sometimes. They've also got hash here, yes sir! A different smoke entirely. . . .

Though we were all agog in Tangier's early morning sun, we noticed our fellow passengers had also picked up an extra piece of Moroccan baggage, like our Mohammed. This tipped us off.

"No, man, we don't want to buy anything," we said firmly.

"One gram, one dirham. Very cheap. Ask anyone, ask any Moroccan, cheap price, no shit." He dipped into his denim jacket and reappeared with a small paper of kif. "One dirham," he announced. One dirham is worth about twenty cents.

"No! Look, man, we don't want to buy _anything_ now. Maybe later," we said.

"Hokay, maybe later," Mohammed agreed, putting away the kif. "You look for house?"

"What?"

"You looking for rent house? I know house, very clean,

nice, very cheap, fifteen, twenty dollar month."

"Look, man, we just want to get to a hotel right now. We don't want to do anything else."

By now we had made it into a small sunny palmtree plaza in front of the train station. Hotel territory.

"OK, come on," Mohammed said. "I take you to nice hotel."

This dude could cut Dale Carnegie with his tongue tied behind his back!

No matter what season you get to Tangier, all the hotels in town are loaded with freaks in every stage of wax and wane. You can meet them all at the Café Central. Just follow your Third Eye to the Casbah.

The fabulous Casbah!

The bloodstream of Arabia.

It's the Middle Ages, the Casbah. Narrow, twisty streets, sudden bends into sunny plazas, hundreds of barefoot children playing in a time machine. Like walking through capillaries.

But you must beware of certain antibodies, which require your consent to work.

Tangier is a small town. Everyone knows everyone. So, by subtraction, anyone they don't know is a tourist-- and they know it. Prepare for pickpockets and be thankful when all you get are hustlers. You'll have a nice ride through the Casbah until you're suddenly eliminated at one end or the other, back in your own century. Spiced out.

Imagine an enormous writhing body swirling fans of yellow, blue and orange flamingo feathers. You get an inkling of the Casbah.

Feel a rich black evening by starshine as you walk a walled Africa street through the shadow of a peaked arch. A single heavy pine door opens into the Sultan's Garden. You smell jasmine. The birds chitter, "Ash breeti, ash breeti. . . ." You see deep black outlines of tall

spreading palms, their dark green tops barely illuminated in Arabian starlight.
    Imagine a rat in the bathroom!

    Within two days we had been warned for and against the Dancing Boy Café. What would you do in our place?

    Dancing Boy Café. Take a special twist in a Casbah alley, enter greendark smokehouse. Joint is loaded. Decorated in Solomon's Seal. Six mint teas, por favor. Scuffle the chairs around.
    A boy sits on a raised platform in the corner. He wears a caftan with a thick dark red felt garter on his hips. A pipe has slithered into your hands.
    The band strikes up a cantata for oud and turtle shells. A dull buzz infiltrates your brains. You pass the pipe.
    An invisible Islamic puppeteer jerks the boy to his feet. He collapses again, begging for just one more pipe. Smokeflash! Pipes jut from all nine orifices of his body. The boy begins to dance. . . .

Rolling, swaying, softly rising
Throbbing black calligraphy;
Liquid sinewave, dark mercury rain. Dance of the
    Dancing Boy . . .
Chocolate ribbon eyes look at YOU!
Felt-gartered hips roll at YOU!
Rolling, swaying, dancing,
Twirling, dancing Dancing Boy!
FASTER, FASTER WHIRLING SWAYING ROLLING DANCING BOY!!
Pipes passing, smoke curling, clapping chanting,
    clapping swaying,
Clapping calling, clapping calling, calling, calling:
    "MAGICIAN!! MAGICIAN!!"
Strange Arab rhythm plucking fevers from thin air,
Pass from hand to hand
They turn to tangerines!
Smell of kif rank, urine stink, sweet mint tea drink.
    END WITH A BANG!!!
Silence.

    Thatsa some cafe! We always went with a guide, or with some multiplying billiard balls.
    The Café Central, which began this discussion, is another saloon entirely. It's in the Zoco Chico. The drainplug on the bathtub of the desert. Why, there are more cafes in the Zoco Chico than in the entire state of New York! If you laid all the cafes in the Zoco Chico end to end they would hatch a plot that reached from Ur to Brasilia!
    The Zoco Chico is nowadays like a dried-up tangerine. A relic of those Bogart days when Tangier was an international currency cesspool, the Zoco sports a zillion hustlers, petty creeps, and police informers. But it's a beautiful place to sit with a mint tea and watch Morocco gush by.
    There are also a few fine hash bars in the Zoco, for which

Morocco is justly famous. We would go in with a regular and get righteously blown out of our skulls. There's so much to do. You can watch TV ("The Berber Rifles vs. The Slug"), or the Arabs doing their unbelievable things, or the opiated bar musicians on a platform in back. Have a sip of opium tea--no more than one if you value your medulla oblongata. Very pleasant way to spend an evening. No purchase necessary.

    Contrary to the fairy tales, Casbahs do not exist by drugs alone. The Casbah is the Arab town. Arabs live here, go to school here, piss, shit, and pray here. They also manufacture everything they need for life--usually out of shoe horns and old gum. And don't think they haven't got lathes, buster! They've got lathes, made out of wood and run with the big toe.

    They got lathes,
    They got looms,
    They got bathyscaphes,
    They got brooms.

    They got picks,
    They got pox,
    They get stoned
    With precious rocks.

    They got tricks,
    They got trauma,
    They got rickets
    And glaucoma.

    Baghdad dynasties give way to oily smiles;
    Blood feuds recompose in strong denials.

The Casbah is just emerging from feudalism, heading straight for Babble-On with a stopover for the Palestine Liberation Organization. Those picturesque narrow streets in Tangier's Casbah are just wide enough to admit a sporty new Fiat.

The trick to the Casbah is trade. The Arabs are handlers. Because of its unique geography, Tangier still thrives as pivotman for the Eurafrica money trade. Here's where the big profits lie. The guys who handle money always have sticky fingers. And, of course, hashish being so resinous, too. . . .

You can buy ingots here--gold or hash, take yer pick. Cash and carry.

Among the Arabs themselves an elaborate credit system accounts for everything from commercial transactions to karma. They haven't found a secret weapon to beat the finance company either: in Arabia, as in America, credit goes to the oldest family on the block.

What with the very agreeable climate here, new deals are sprouting all the time and no one seems to go hungry. Even so, Tangier hasn't been able to ransom itself from the traditional Arab plague of eye and throat diseases. There's more to money than meets the rent.

Always in the back of our minds is this: What can we learn from Morocco to bring the capitalists to their knees, purify the air and water, and get the whole earth onto one together vibration? In Tangier we learn that even though they kicked out the French, they still love to talk with rounded lips; even though the old wrinkled men can make it by handcraft, the young machos are looking at Hondas.

By the same token, we sure would like to learn to make one of those hand lathes.

Before we came to Tangier we figured the mutual dope scene would create a bond between Arabia and America. This perhaps was our biggest illusion. Arabs smoke dope, all right, but Tangier is a hustle market clear through. No ceremonial smoking. After all, they've been doing it for four thousand years in North Africa. Ain't no big thing to them.

But they found out that American longhairs will steal the family jools for a lump of green glop, and the unity of opposites is put to a practical test. With traditional Old World charm they shrewdly diddle every dude off the boat, relying on darkness and the Stock Exchange to conceal their sleight-of-hand.

Now, of course, one can score some good shit here. If you just hang around a while someone will lay some on you. But personally I wouldn't figure on doing a deal that will set Interpol back 250 years, unless you're a PRO.*

Here are some authoritative Morocco dope notes. After all, what trail are we on, anyway? It is still a fact that most freaks come to Tangier hypnotized by lurid tales of druggee.

As I said, kif is the Moroccan national smoke. It's made from the flowering tops of your old pal cannabis sativa. You mix it with cuttings from the roots. You always see it clean-- no stems or seeds. You smoke it like tobacco. Do not hold it down in your lungs, or you'll go on a wild stomach trip. It gives you a good rush for a few minutes. Then you smoke some more.

Kif costs about one dirham per gram, regardless of quantity. But the more you buy . . . the more likely you will hear from a certain Inspector Soussi of the Central Police Station.

Contrary to popular belief, dope is illegal in Morocco. Kif and marijuana are classified as "poisonous substances." Any crime connected with kif can get you six days to two months in jail and a fine of $24 to $720. To my knowledge, no American has ever actually been busted for kif in Morocco. Sometimes a Moroccan will get busted for dealing huge quantities. They like to stuff 144,000 kilos into the stomachs of 656 camels and move the train across the desert. The cops get tipped off when a camel drops dead at the market. So an American with his dirham bag is pretty puny shit.

Under Moroccan law, hashish is distinguished from kif or marijuana. Don't ask me why. Hash counts as a "narcotic,"

---

*But for you Pro's, Interpol is a big shuck. You imagine a global organization with graying chieftains headquartered in Paris communicating with a world net of highly trained agents?

Ho, ho, ho!

It's really a storefront schlock joint that sends a tin badge to the rawest rookie on each city's police force.

along with opium, heroin, and soma. Many Moroccans think hash drives you mad. Maybe they're right, judging from some of the freaks here. . . . There's the hash freak who jumped out of the window and broke into pieces on the rue de la Plage, and the one who tried to do himself in with a huge Berber shank, and I got a million stories. Anyway, possession or dealing hash can get you three months to two years in the joint, and a fine of $240 to $2400. Americans <u>do</u> occasionally get busted for hash.

If you buy a large stash of hash in Tangier--more than just personal smoking shit--you run a fair chance of getting busted. I personally know several street hustlers who have turned in Americans they themselves sold hash to. The hustlers get the dope back, collect a reward from the ubiquitous Inspector Soussi, and keep the bread the American fish paid.

The reason for this shocking practice is this: if you buy a lot of dope, the Moroccans figure you want to deal. If <u>you</u> want to deal, you're stealing the action from some Moroccan. They've had a lot of experience with foreign exploitation. Hip imperialism is no different.

But then, there is Ahmed. Ahh, yes. Ahmed. The Dope Czar of Africa. His shop sits right behind the American Cultural Center. All work guaranteed. They reckon Ahmed is just about as powerful as the Chief of Police around here. And just about as expensive:

Dope Czar of Africa;
Hash and acid trafficker.
Hand in glove of Yankee doeskin,
Debtor of the Phoenician Public Pest Law.

He sold British when she mandated;
Rolled the French in their own <u>bicot</u>!
Incarceration antedated
By Royal Decree Seisenta y nueve Seisenta y ocho.

The Heavyweight Champeen Dope Dealer. Citation from the Sultan of Ketama. Claims with equanimity to being third-eye adept, ex-Seabee, correspondent for La Nación, or what-have-you.

Smokes from a long silver pipe studded with rubies and emeralds. But you'll note he only smokes kif off the top of pipes of hash he fixes for prospective customers. He won't touch hash.

During the day he's just another street freak you see in the Zoco. At night, he turns into Ahmed the King. Many want to film him, or some goddamned thing.

"Buy from Ahmed," he says with a liquid wave, "and every border you cross will be free!"

There's a veiled threat there somewhere.

Somehow we had it in our heads that Arabs get Section 8 deferments from the laws of history. On the boat we fantasized about "sitting around in the coffeehouses all day long getting high," or being beckoned by veiled women, or the Walled Garden of Truth.

And the thing is, we _found_ all those things! There _are_ walled gardens of truth, and all the women _are_ veiled, and they _do_ sit around and get high all day long. _All_ those things _really_ happen. But they are commonplace! Reality fills out, abhorring the vacuums of fantasy.

On this level, for us, it resolved into an economic scene. You have to deal with this hip imperialism thing. You have to deal with hustling. You have to deal with men who hold their cocks and spit at you.

Some freaks deal with it by buying a Moroccan robe, two kilos of hash, and "going Arab." This is a good willed but futile racist guilt trip, in my opinion. For one thing, they don't usually learn more than ten words of Arabic. It takes the most guts of all just to be your real self here. You can still learn Arabic.

I forbear to point out that the Arabs know jive when they see it.

I must say, in fact, that we don't know many Americans in Morocco who really have it together. Strung out. Looking for some gig, for some culture they can adopt, or one that will adopt them. That is a very tough scene. The only people the Arabs adopt are former colonial administrators who have a karmic link and a political whip--like T. E. Lawrence and Marshal Lyautey.* (Of course, there's always the outlaw genius--like Sir Richard Burton.)

The Arabs tend to act that way historically. They absorb other cultures at the interfaces rather than implant their own. This is commendable, but it tends to make Arabs among the most severely colonized people on earth. Americans are drilling for oil in Algeria. Where does a hippie get off trying to fit in?

Dig Max, for instance. L.A. nouveau hip. Read a book once about pentacles. Jowls. Smiles by scraping his front teeth. Ran into him the first time when our guard was down and he was looking for a house.

> Scene: Morning in Arabia. We are watching
> a line of Arabs, bent backs, trudging, ball-
> and-chained. Hod-carriers, we believe.
> Long black car slowly prowling alongside.
> Sunglasses in back seat pulls back the window
> curtain to fire a flameburst from his Super-8,

---

*Lyautey was French Colonial administrator of Morocco and a renowned Arabist-cum-pig. He is one of the few non-Muslims ever allowed to visit Mecca. They invited him to kiss the sacred Kaba'a, but "in a magnanimous display of statesmanship" he symbolically kissed the top of the temple stairs instead.

which is designed as an expensive movie camera.

MAX (from behind): Hey, man! Far out! Know of any groovy pads for rent? (Gives the hippie handshake.)

ME (thinking): Fascism or feudalism? (Speaking) European section, or Casbah?

MAX: It don't matter to me, man. Anything's faar-fucking-out!! (We walk a bit.) Hey-y, man. Had any of the brown semolina yet? Good substitute for brown rice.

ME: No. It's good, is it?

MAX: Yeah, man. We cook it every morning at sunrise. (We walk a bit more.) Say-y, man. Bought any dope from Ahmed yet? He's really outasight, man. Yessir. Ol' Three Eye!

ME: Hm.

MAX: Never pass his place without I genuflect. Say! Do you smoke?

ME: What do you mean?

MAX (irritated): You know, man, do you _smoke_. Grass, hash--psychedelic _drugs_. _You_ know.

ME: Well, yeah, I like to get high.

MAX: Well, you never know. (We walk a bit more.) Say, man! You ever read any Krishnamurti?

At this point I pull a brightly colored silk
from a secret pocket and put a month between
Max and me. Next meeting, by accident, I
nearly don't recognize him, since he's wearing
a robe and walking with an Arab slouch.

MAX: Say-y-y. Sorry I didn't see you sooner.
  Learned any Arabic yet?

ME: Some. Whatever's hip, eh, Max?

MAX: Hey, man, I'd like you to meet my slouch.

SLOUCH: Sbaa'kher. La bess?

ME: Hamdullah.

SLOUCH: Al-loora al-arbiya wached el-msla
  deeal notk.

ME: NAHAL'BAK!! And fuck off to you too, Max!

MAX: Aslamma! (Exits in direction of American
  Express.)

                    CURTAIN

You'd think the fucker discovered Arabia or something!
We met one Max type in Marrakech who changed his name from
Milton to Eric and now was getting all the girls. Took his
picture to sell to the back cover of comic books.
  The Max age is usually around nineteen. There's an
elder hip crowd in town reminiscent of beatniks. Been out
of the States for ten years. Regularly make it to Tangier

to work on that novel. Confused about money and bewildered by the new generation.

Mike. Harvard, Class of '57. Ex-ghost writer for UNESCO. "When I left Harvard, I knew more than anyone else. Now, you guys know more than me!" Plans to go to the States to see what he's been reading about in the <u>Herald Tribune</u>. (He still calls it the <u>Paris Herald</u>. Has never set foot outside New York, but knows Berkeley is a must see.

Living with this Swedish woman, but still married, see, with two kids, makes it hard to get welfare in the States, huh? Ahh, mumble, fucked up, mnmmm Tangier (makes a creaking sound like stopping your glottis without taking in any air and saying "nnnnn") y'knowmmmmnm RIP VAN WINKLE!

Just the exact opposite of Max. A ginger man of letters. Tangier's got a pipeful of 'em. Just now he's working on a novel, but his next book will be about the Hashish Trail. . . . In the meantime he's got to get that mumble visa for his y'know mnmmmchick, fucking consulate man mnm always give you shit about everything rnrmnm. . . .

Max and Mike. Mike and Max. They don't know each other--not yet--but they'll meet at the Café Central. They both have indefinite plans and drink bottled water. Max lives in the Casbah (he found a pad!). Mike recently moved out of it into an apartment in the Portuguese quarter.* NVMS. No visible means of support. Probably living off dowry, or Defense Department grant, or inheritance. Working both sides of the generation gap. Private survival at the People's expense? We'd better call in a karmaccountant.

---

*In 1661, Catherine of Braganza, princess of Portugal, married Charles II, king of England, bringing Tangier as her dowry.

So what's the story anyway? Who are these Arab folk, and what about the Berber Rifles? How did Max's nose get into their business?

No one knows. Bullet-brained geopoliticos think they originated maybe around Yemen somewhere? Or Abu Dhabi? With names like that it's safe to speculate. But when they finally conquered their way to Morocco (707 A.D.) the Arabs found the Berbers already there, fiercely muttering in their beards. The conquerors would ask, "Where you come from?" The natives would just wave vaguely toward the mountains. Like the Incas. They even had knot writing, he quipued.

The Arabs sidled up to the Berbers, much as they do to Americans now, to let them in on this groovy new deal called Islam. "Why not?" figured the Berbers. "They can't read our knot writing anyway. And besides, they didn't bring any women along. We can send some of ours over to find out what's really what."

The Arabs naturally wanted to know how much Berber nooky was going to cost. The Berbers just laughed. The Arabs got offended and showed the soles of their feet. The Berbers pissed on them. The Arabs attacked, furious. The Berbers defended. Finally, the Arabs pulled out their Haroun el-Raschid Gatling Gun and mowed them back to the mountains. But no one-- not even the Caliph of Baghdad--gets the Berbers out of the mountains!

So they struck a de facto deal. Arabs in the valleys, Berbers in the mountains.

The Arabs soon hustled some women in from Baghdad so they could get on with the Empire. Before the Berbers knew it, their conquerors had stitched up Morocco tight for Islam and were already on the boat for Spain. The mountain people shrugged, and planted more Bedouin Black.

After a spell the Arabs met up with some tough customers at the gates of Paris: the Frankish Crusaders. They were eventually driven back across the Strait of Gibraltar and had to be content with the entire known world from Morocco to Malaya. Not a bad haul, even by today's high standard of hegemony.

In Morocco itself the Berbers allowed as how Islam was all right and why make trouble. The Arabs had enough sense to see they'd better get on the good side of the mountain people

or else they could expect some night raiding. So they made
another deal.

"You Berbers fix us some eats and we'll make sure no one
bothers you," said the Arabs, with their fingers crossed just
in case.

The Berbers answered, "OK, OK," wishing they'd go home.
These Arabs were getting to be a nuisance. No one had bothered
them before except for a few Romans or Vandals who couldn't
climb mountains anyhow.

"Just sign here . . . thank you!" and the Arabs sank back
onto their poufs and had another pipe. Many years later they
built some tin towns for Berbers who wanted to live near Arab
cities. And of course, they taught them arithmetic.

Eventually white men got involved, through the use of
zero as a place holder. When Portuguese, English, and Spanish
crossed the Strait to worm the secret out of the Arabs, some
Berber chieftains even defended!

As every schoolboy knows, however, the Europeans had a coat
of arms and what could mere Arabs do? They learned to speak
Spanish and told the Berbers to roll with the punches. That
remains the situation to this day.

Other important developments were the invention of
travelogs and the birth of Arthur Frommer. Tangier is the
only North African city in Europe On Five Dollars A Day.
William Burroughs had something to do with it too.

If you've ever seen "Casablanca" you know about Morocco's
modern history. Foreign diplomats resided in Tangier because
it was easy to split from. Excellent reasoning. The black
market drew a shitload of adventure heads and slimy capitalists.
End of the war--Pif! The swine were left with a fistful of
dirhams, blinking in the bright lights of the Café de France,
while the Pigs set off for Indochina.

Basically, it's a fine place, Tangier. For a while,
anyway. Gets a little seedy if you stay too long. The best
thing about it is totally unknown: the Atlantic beaches near
town are out of sight!! We would hitchhike twelve miles west,
out to Cap Spartel, to absolutely the best beach we've ever
seen! (And that includes L.A., Greece, Capri, Yugoslavia,
Mexico and the ridiculous south of France!) They call it
Robinson's Beach.

Just across the road from Robinson's is another fantastic

beach. No name. It looks onto some Phoenician ruins and the Caves of Hercules. You can climb through incredible tide pools that look like the surface of Jupiter or watch Atlantic liners hazy on the bright horizon plying between Lisbon and Dakar. It's the coast of Africa, me hearties!!

Want to hear some poetry composed out at the beach?

>
> The Will of the People,
> Being stronger than
>   the Man's Tricknology,
> Perhaps needs a little shock treatment:
> An electrode here,
> A free lunch there. . . .
> For that alone which is ungovernable
> Is Nature's great abundance.
>
> Waves of Revolution
> (Forms of evolution)
> Ride the killer surf
> To a warm sea beach--
> Tide pools, shell stars,
> The Whole System.
> (Only, watch for the next big wave
> Whose authority is the Principle of Change.)

Nine waves on, nine waves off. Nature's rule of thumb.

The Berber town attached to Tangier, on the road to Tetuan, is called Beni Makada. They don't get much traffic out in Berber country, which is stone beautiful country.

One day we picked up a Berber hitchhiking and took him through the mountains, round multifold bends and crannies, past an enchanted castle, clear down to where the road peters out into a goat track. If we hadn't happened by, he would have walked it--a distance of about thirty-five miles!

Everything east of Tangier is Berber country--the rugged

Rif mountains, vaguely reminiscent of the Sierras, the hilly meadow switchbacks patched with grazing camels and lone herdsmen, chubby women wearing red-and-white striped bustled skirts. They are Jbala--mountain people. They know more than you, me, and Mike put together. "My dear fellow, I'm afraid we're two centuries ahead of them, although they're two centuries behind us, I admit."

Berbers get a special chapter, but I will say that in the last few years the Peace Corps has been teaching them agriculture, which situation is certainly a candidate for Dubious Achievement of the Millenium.

Apropos a final observation. The latest foreign invader to sully Tangier's shore is your old fiend Armorica. Barbara Hutton, world's richest woman, is their cover. She has a huge house in the Casbah with underground monorail to the old American Legation, now the Arabic Language School. The U.S. consul in Algiers was trained here. The American School is being taken over by the State Department. The U.S. Consulate owns two huge hills in Souani quarter being readied for the University of North Africa. The chief of the Foreign Buildings Office--the FBO--from Tangier went on special assignment as ambassador to Somali, which just happened to have a pro-Mao countercoup a few days later.

The former chief agent of the CIA in Prague is now regional manager for Pfizer International in Casablanca. The ambassador to Somali's son plays golf with the king's brother. The Deputy Director of AID interviews prospective teachers at the American School. It's the Whole Hog.

On the plus side, every once in a while you'll see some J'lallah dancers. We saw them on May 25, Mohammed's birthday. They belong to a far-out sect of whirling--that's right, whirling--dervishes. On Mohammed's birthday they dance until they drop.

More whirling and other dervishes, acrobats, fortunetellers, hashish eaters, and Arabian Nights down in the fabled red city of Marrakech.

III

MARRAKECH: CERTIFICATE "X"

>Marrakech. What could be nicer? Hip barter in full swing. Basic unit of exchange: amount of time you stay stoned. Big mug of opium tea worth a thimbleful of great hash.
>   Hash cookies a whammo! item here. Bring harmonica.
>   Beautiful red city ringed with blue-white mountains. The American Dream.
>
>   --Notebook Entry

"Yore in Yogurt Culture!" Making music in Marrakech. We even took the Marrakech Express down from Casablanca. Zingo!--the Jesus Christ the <u>Casbah!</u> Saw all our friends from the boat. Dope until we didn't. Rave reviews!!
   Nighttime in the Jamaa el-F'na. The Meeting Place of the

Dead. The port of the desert. Bedouins, Berbers, and billiard markers. Gnaoui dancers from Mauritania. Acrobats, jugglers, storytellers. Watersellers wrapped in red, toting goatskin bags with golden faucets. "Hey meester! How much for lady??" Let your imagination run stark raving wild and you'll get the idea.

Remember all those old Buster Crabbe flicks? The French Foreign Legion and all? Well, Marrakech is the place the Bedouins were always trying to make it to. The desert is like an ocean of sand and Marrakech is the western port. The Arabs navigate the Sahara like the English ruled the sea.

Do you want to buy figs? Do you want to silkscreen resin from raw hash plants? Do you want a slave, or want to give one up? Are you addicted to anything? "Go to the Gran' Place, m'sieu." Are you hungry, thirsty or curious? Could you dig a man with microscope eyes or a woman selling herbs and ointments? Astringent of <u>polygonum erectum</u>? A fortuneteller from Spain or dancers from Sudan, acrobats from Senegal, magicians from Iran? The sheikh, the Sufi, the sage? The wit? The wizard? The keys to the kingdom?

WELL??
IT'S ON THE DRUM!!
THE JAMAA EL-F'NA IS THE PLACE!!
THE HIGHWAY 61 OF AFRICA!
OVER FOUR THOUSAND YEARS OF BONDED SERVICE!

Your Storytellers in Action

Once a Finn and a Swiss came to Marrakech to score some shit. They stopped the first passerby they encountered.

"Hey, man, do you know where we can score some shit?" the Swiss opened.

"Yeah, some <u>real</u> shit. Not this horseshit or

camelshit they give you!" the Finn echoed.

"You mean some real, honest to God SHIT?" the passerby inquired with a smile, knowing. "Follow me!"

They walked down a broad palmlined avenue, whose villas and walls were salmon red.

"Agadir," the Swiss was saying.

"Essaouira," echoed the Finn.

"Been there myself," the passerby nodded pleasantly.

They turned into a park that fronted on the corner of the Jamaa el-F'na.

"I know a guy," the passerby was saying.

"Ahh," responded the Finn.

Likewise the Swiss: "Ohh!"

They crossed into the Jamaa, eyes sweeping the cafes. They didn't even seem to notice the snake charmers and acrobats.

"Wait here," the passerby said, indicating a brass plate in the ground. To make doubly sure, he riveted the foreigners to the spot.

"Piss on Swiss and Sin on Finn!!" the passerby crowed hysterically, ripping off a plastic mask to reveal the face of a <u>Passerby</u>: one of those hideous fanatical Berber tribesmen who masquerade as capitalist dogs! The Swiss and Finn tried with all their might to get loose, but the rivets held fast! The Passerby was doing strange dances, jumping on both feet while touching his finger tip to a dagger point!

Somehow a BBC stringer wormed his way into the crowd and he asked that they hold off a sec until he telephoned his bureau. They smiled at his accent and agreed with a bow.

Suddenly, the Government turned off all the lights, to save on electricity! The Passerby was foiled! The rivets broke loose and the Europeans were set free!

The music started up once more. It had all been a big joke or something.

Marrakech is surrounded by twenty miles of palm forest. A red plop with a big green ring. Come in a little closer and you see the red plop is veined with green blotches. Close in more and you realize most of the city is actually green. The red lines throw such a powerful aura they tint the whole picture.
 A little closer, please. Whoops--watch it!

 Scene: Swarthy Arab grabs your elbow, spins you round and round and pulls collapsible table from folds of his robe. Crowd forms instantly. You are in the center. Ten-dirham note is sticking mysteriously from your hand. The Arab strokes a leather belt. He cracks it, doubles it over, and coils it up.

ARAB: Keep ten, you give me five! (He shoves the coiled belt toward you.)

YOU: Hey, what's this, what's this all about, man? (You are surprised he knows your language.)

CROWD (drowning you out): Come on, man, keep ten, you give him five!

YOU (looking at the ten in your hand): Hey, no, man, I don't want to do this. . . . (You try to hand the note to an Arab in the crowd.)

The performing Arab offers the coiled belt to the
crowd. Another Moroccan sticks his finger into
one of the two loops formed in the center. The
first Arab slowly uncoils the belt. The second's
finger "catches" the loop. He wins ten dirham.
General excitement.

ARAB (to YOU): Keep ten, you give me five. Put your
   finger in.

He ever so slowly coils the belt up again. It is
perfectly obvious which loop to "catch" and which
to avoid.

   Oh, Lordy, Lordy, the Jamaa el-F'na. What doesn't go
down there?!

Scene: Red-fezzed, white-robed, brown-faced LUNAR
LORD stands in front of Arab anatomy chart. A
crowd gathers like an oyster round a pearl. Native
bearers bring in a sickling on a howdah. LUNAR
has a look. Consults a star.

LUNAR LORD (chanting): Al-lah, Al-lah,
                        Keewatin Dudeney;
                        Al-lah, Al-lah,
                        Riboflavin scrutiny!

Passes his moonbeam hands over the sickling's legs.

Dips fingers into clear water and throws droplets
at a hunk of raw mutton. Brushes sickling's
aura with two stork feathers.)

SICKLING (screams): AIEEE!!!

LUNAR LORD (makes the call of a bird and the cry
   of a wolf): Brrt! Ow-wo-wooo! (Takes a
   mouthful of clear water and sprays it on sickling.)

SICKLING (smiling): Ahhh. (He is cured.)

    As much going on in the Jamaa el-F'na as in Berkeley!
Dispatched a radiogram thus to the Chamber of Commerce.

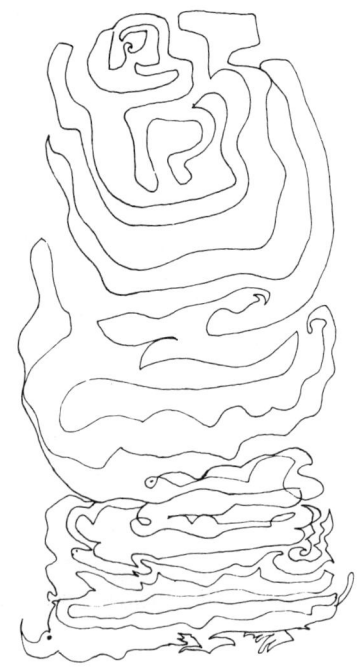

MARRAKECH, By MR. FIRST-NIGHTER

The main arteries of the medina stretch into the Jamaa el-F'na like giant feed tubes. "Medina" is what they call the Casbah in Marrakech. It means "town" in Arabic. "Casbah," that exotic Arabian vision, actually comes from Spanish.

You hear a lot of people asking, "Gee, wonder what it would be like to <u>live</u> in the medina!" Well, it just so happens that foreign art<u>ists</u> can cop free housing from the government. Right in the middle of the medina, either in Marrakech or Fez. How about that? Before we knew it, we were safely in the care of Hizzoner the Inspector of Historic Monuments in Marrakech, and domiciled--that is, enthroned--in the SULTAN'S PALACE!!

No shit!

The Sultan's Palace is the living center of the medina. Tourists rarely venture back there. Afraid of the slave market.

Actually, we just had a wing of the Palace. Not the whole thing. We asked for the whole thing, but they apologized that the government still likes to do business there, if we didn't mind.

Our wing was completely surrounded by a thirty-foot wall, salmon red. Directions: Go into the medina from the Jamaa el-F'na, walk straight on until you come to a high wall. Follow the wall--no matter what--until you come to a big pine door. It's the only door in the whole wall. Number 75, Bahia Palace. Knock loud, and come any time.

The thick door double locked us into a huge blackbird garden, spreading hundred-foot palms sweeping the sky, flame-red geraniums, purple-yellow banana trees, climbing vines with droopy blue blossoms. An honest to God tropical paradise, take it or leave it.

For your private parts there was even a shower, toilet, running water, and a huge outdoor stone sink. We had complete privacy except for a neighbor three times a week. He was a Moroccan musician and Koranic scholar. Among other things, he composed music in Braille! He had some far out Ministry of Culture gig--the circuit music teacher between Rabat and Marrakech.

We became good friends, and he often serenaded us with Arab, Andalou, and ancient music. There's a music lesson farther on in the journey.

Night got to follow day, and day to follow night. Acute sense of flow along the time stream. Arabian dawn, blackbird garden, Africa night music, serene visits. Occasional warm rain, birds chitter and play, then the monsoon, or mistral, or something: a dark menacing sky, long, looping slash-to-bits raindrops, a vee of razorwing. The sirocco.

Walking naked in a walled garden. Starlight wedges through the palms. A single flute at sweet distance. This is the Garden of Truth.

Take notes for an encyclopedia of psychic cookery. Assume philosophical proportions. Lay bare the reality of garden variety existence. Ride the wind of Nature's secret.

A Search for Sufis?   Spix Fix Hix Trix!!

A search for Sufis led to a self-addressed envelope.
"A Search For Ṣufis," by Dr. T. Lobsang Smythe-Ffrench.
A search for Sufis in the British Museum was respectfully suggested.
A search for Sufis on the Armed Forces Network?
A search for Sufis really brought us to Morocco. Find another way, by Jesus. There must be one. "What is your alternative?" the Pigs would ask as they frisked you.
What the hell are Sufis, I can almost hear you ask. Before we came to Morocco I surely would have said in my hippest manner: "Oh, you know, man, Arabian wise men, magicians, you know." By the time this comes out CBS will probably have a ninety-minute series called "The Sufis." A chi-chi AM pop group will sing "I Ain't Got No Use For Your Christians And Jews." The carefully barbered shaman from Props will rise from his meditation to intone solemnly: "Why

talk of dough when the object is breadmaking?" (Or what about a spinoff called "The Diabolists," maybe starring Charles Manson? Don't put it past CBS!)

What I mean to say is, let's get rid of all foolish notions about wise men. It's another media hype. The fact is (my credentials, sir) that we Americans don't know zhit (squeak) about what's really happening with . . . uh . . . world progress.

Living in a land full of garbage and hatred makes it hard to touch the earth and get in tune. Mind pollution sets in. The psychic senses are the first to die. Believe me--this is the Walled Garden speaking.

One night a bunch of folk were gathered round in the garden. Let's see, there was Jim, the harmonica heir, and he brought along this Armenian writer, Richard, with his friends--Larbi (a Moroccan Berber) and two English dudes. Also Marty and Sue, friends from the boat (the dropout millionaire and wife).

Talk naturally turned to Sufis, what with harmonica and magic tricks and a little dopez-vous. This Richard dude said some good guck. At first, I thought it was just crypto-spiritual bullshit, but I have since come to take things as they are given. It went something like this:

Scene: The Walled Garden. The dope flows.
A group of nine sit in a high-ceilinged room decorated with bright yellow-and-red rugs from Rabat, antique orange clay vases from the camel market, and modern photos of domed mosques and tattooed Berber women. It is one of those magical doper's nights when the words are melody to the vibes.
    JIM, the harmonica heir, is talking to me about spiritual matters.

JIM: Hey, man, have you had any luck with finding Sufis yet?

ME: I'm still looking.

JIM: How about you, Richard? Have you met any
   Sufis?

JIM has been trying to bring RICHARD and ME
   together, us both being writers and linguists.
   We are wary, sniffing each other's assholes.

RICHARD (in a slow voice): None other than we . . .
   ourselves.

Everyone acts like they have thrips or something.

   Later that night, Richard slipped me a piece of paper with
the Arabic alphabet written around the edges, and in the middle
it said: "Whosasufi? Woolpullers." I mulled that one over
for some time.

   Soon afterward we started to learn about "the women."
It came up one night when we were into some opium tea. "The
women" are herbalists. You can get opium pods from "a woman"
(which is what brought it up) or you can get voodoo wax. You
can find "a woman" on every block, if you look sharp.
   If an Arab wife thinks her husband is making it somewhere
else, she might go to "a woman" to concoct something to make
him impotent. If his lover couldn't figure out why he was
suddenly impotent, she might go to "a woman" to get a few
things that would give him a perpetual hard-on. Then all the
women would be satisfied.
   Moroccan men have it all over women when it comes to law,
custom, and property. But they live in mortal fear of poison.
   If the husband has committed a domestic felony, the wife
and "the woman" enter into a black pact. They will make a wax

image of the husband, engraving his name and his mother's name on the front with a wax-handled knife. "The woman" will then smite off a limb. The husband will be unable to use the corresponding limb!

And for the Big One, they will make a wax likeness of the unfortunate fellow and engrave on it the "seven signs," the husband's name, and his mother's name. They then gouge out the eyes with two palm-wood points. They throw the whole mess into a terra-cotta pot of quicklime, toss in a sprig of charib el-h'amam, and bury it near a fire. If the husband somehow atones within seven days, the wife can heal him by digging it up and dunking it in pure water. But after seven days--that's all, gentlemen.

Most Moroccans know something of the black art. Let's say someone's bothered by demons. He might visit "a woman" to pick up some smoq. That's an ink made from wool immersed in pure water, rose water, and saffron water. He would take it to write a formula called el-herz, for which he would also hit up "the woman" for some gazelleskin parchment and a silver box.

The word "talisman" is Arabic. El-herz is a far out talisman to the sun, made up of two parts: the da'oua and the djedouel. The da'oua is a magical verse chant: prayers, appeals, and magical names. It always reaffirms the basic root of Islam, called the shahadah--the witness. "La ilaha il'Allah oo M'hamd urrasululah!" Roughly, "There is no god but God and Mohammed is his Prophet," with a pun on "Mohammed." The djedouel is written, and looks like this:

Key to the Djedouel of the
Da'ouat Ech Shems*

First line: Six signs, written in a special magical script called
  "lunettes." In Arabic, this line is called "seb'a Khouatim."
  They conjure this particular djedouel. The lunettes characters
  are believed by some Arabic scholars to be of Hebraic origin.
  To me, they resemble the code in Conan Doyle's The Case of the
  Dancing Men.
Second line: The Seven Signs.
Third line: Seven letters of the alphabet. Fâ, djim, chin, thâ,
  zâ, khâ, zin. These are the only letters not found in the
  first seven verses of the first sura of the Koran ("fâtih'a").
  They have magical properties and are called "saouâquit el-fâtih'a."
Fourth line: Seven particularly powerful names for Allah. Fard
  (unique), djebbar (all-powerful), shakdar (forgiving), thâbit
  (firm), z'ahir (evident), khabîr (vigilant), zakî (pure).
Fifth line: The Seven Spirits. In Arabic, "er roûh'âniyya es seb'a."
  They are Roûquiâil, Djebriâil, Semsemâil, Dabkhaail, Cerfiâil,
  Aniâil, Kesfiâil.
Sixth line: The seven princes of the djouns. They are Moudhhib,
  Merra, Ah'mar, Borquân, Chemhoûrech, Aliod', Mîmoûn. These names
  are very important in Muslim magic.
Seventh line: The seven days of the week.
Eighth line: The Seven Sacred Planets (corresponding to the days).
  Shems, Quamar, Mirrîkh, Out'ârid, Mouchtarî, Zohra, Zouh'al.

---

*The Arab writes from right to left.

Magic is indisputable and indispensable in Morocco. But does that mean everyone's a Sufi?

On doorways in the medina you will see a red hand. This is a very powerful Arab talisman and using it means you're into some pretty way out magical practice. The "hand of Fatima" is also tattooed between the eyes of a great number of Moroccan women. The hand means three things to these warrior kings--an invocation of Allah, for one. A commentator on the Koran says: "If you would invoke Allah, show him the palms of your hands. When you have finished, pass your hands in front of your face." Second, a living symbol of the Law of Islam. The hand has five fingers with three joints each, except the thumb with two. These symbolize the five fundamental cornerstones of Islam, which each have three amendments (except for the first, which only has two). All five tenets are rooted in and extensions of Allah, the stock of the hand. Thus, to ward off the evil eye, an Arab will shield his face with his hand, palm outward, fingers spread. Third, of course, the hand is the traditional defense against enemies of all kinds.

All Arabs are into this hand magic. But clearly, all are not Sufis. No street hustler who turns in his customers could be a Sufi. No one that pinches Barbara's ass could be a Sufi. Nevertheless, they _are_ into this practical, nuts-and-bolts magic. For proof, put a curse on one of their fathers and watch them flip out.

So whosasufi? "Suf" in Arabic means "wool." Ahmed Sefrioui, the Minister of Culture and well-known Moroccan author, says he knows one in Fez, but he's old and very hard to find. A friend of mine who claims to know says "Murcía," but Sefrioui says Murcía is bogus. "Too stoned," he says slyly. "Black magician." In fact, every Sufi-sighting (at this stage) gets countered by another, claiming a bigger and better spiritual enlightenment!

This may be a built-in safeguard of the Sufi system. Or, it may be that all the Sufi sects really like to badmouth one another. At one time the Muslims themselves outlawed Sufism in the Maghreb, asserting it denies some of the laws of Mohammed.

But I think the point is that real Sufis don't advertise. Some of them don't even know they _are_ Sufis! This is documented in countless Sufi teaching tales.

In fact, but for those teaching tales, you might think the whole thing was a hype of the Middle East Press Agency.

The Sufis happen to have just about the richest and most incredible poetic literature of all time. This should settle any doubts as to authenticity. The literature consists of oral teaching stories and epic poems. The greatest of all Sufi poets, by unanimous acclaim, was the Afghani Jalaluddin Rumi. (And mind you, Omar Khayyam was also a Sufi!)

Rumi wrote the <u>Mathnawi</u> (Spiritual Couplets) and <u>Fihi Ma Fihi</u> (In It What Is <u>In It</u>). Rumi's stories, along with numberless other Sufi tales in all their variations, are still extremely popular throughout the entire Arabic-speaking world. You run across them in coffeehouses, in sitting rooms, in hash bars, and naturally in the Jamaa el-F'na.

Scene: Jamaa el-F'na, four P.M. Psychic clock chiming. Twenty thousand Afro-Arabian souls working flexors. Snake charmers, witches, and winnowing fans, <u>in broad daylight</u>. We are traveling <u>incognito, disguised</u> as mechanical chess players. We pass a squatting ARAB flying a red kite scrawled with Arabic writing.

WE: What's that say on the kite?

SQUATTING ARAB: "Parable Of The Three Domains!"

WE: Well, what's this all about, anyway?

ARAB: I'm advertising for two storytellers.

WE: And where might they be found, my good man?

He points.

We walk in the direction of the storytellers. The

biggest crowd? Of course! A nearly nude desert SAGE, brown as the soles of his feet, sits crosslegged beside a three-foot tall hookah. Doves perch on his shoulders and walk nonchalantly through an obstacle course of plastic flowers stuck into Coca-Cola cans. The SAGE looks about like any Berkeley or Greenwich Village freak: very long fuzzy hair, wild brown eyes.

He is shouting. All ears a-cock, across the Coke garden, squats a cartoon EGG with missing teeth. Somehow, he's getting down the hot peanut candy.

SAGE (in translation): Dammit, I tell you the Prophet spoke with God ninety thousand times and when he got back the bed was still warm!

EGG: Man, you crazy, you flipped out, you gay, you Jewish, you sick, you middle class, you drug addict, you ex-con, you too dramatic! You fucked up!

SAGE: Ahh, you bloody heathen! I spit in the milk of your mother! I this and that on your this! Do what's _right_, motherfucker! Put your head into this jug of herbal water!

He picks up an engraved golden cauldron and shoves it in the direction of EGG. Some herbal water splashes a dove, but it rolls off his back.

EGG (suspicious but self-confident): OK, smartass, I will. But don't forget that I know Yoga.

He sends a team of four doves to fetch the jug, which SAGE has put into a dove cart.

SAGE (mutters): I'll make you eat your words through your skin, Jewbag! (Roars.) LA ILAHA IL'ALLAH OO M'HAMD URRASULULAH!! (Lowers a wing.) Uh . . . care for a pipe, old man?

EGG: Don't mind if I do.

They go through a doves-and-pipes routine. SAGE shoots EGG the evil eye; EGG defends with spread fingers. EGG shoots it back; SAGE defends likewise. EGG picks up a dove that is inspecting a nearby vase of clove orange. He sets the bird onto his left hand for a moment, takes his right hand away and--Presto! A small pipe sits where the dove just sat, puffing little smoke rings!

CROWD: Murmur! Murmur!

EGG: I thank you! I thank you! You are too kind! Thank you very much!

CROWD: Don't thank us, thank Allah!

SAGE: Bah! Flummery! Two bit conjuring! He did it with the peanut candy! Plain as the egg on his face! You want to see something? Look at <u>this</u>!

The desert SAGE picks up a small pipe and clasps it in his two outstretched hands. He closes his hands a moment, then opens them to reveal a dove fluttering its wings. It is quite beautiful.

CROWD: Bismillah! Hamdullah!

SAGE (blushing modestly): You are very kind. . . .

EGG: Black thread! Black thread! Who couldn't do that if they had some black thread?

SAGE: OK, so we're even Steven. Enough juggling. Let's have that pipe now and get on with it.

EGG: Right. (He gets up and crosses the midden over to the huge hookah.)

SAGE (lighting some incense from Mecca, the kind you burn outdoors): Well, Egg? You ready to get a bird tied round your neck?

EGG (takes a huge hit off the hookah): Yeahhh. Sock it to me, man.

The SAGE dunks the EGG head into the cauldron of lilac water. He holds it under for a few seconds, then takes it out.

SAGE: H'mm?

EGG (roars): SON OF A DOG!! CURSED SWINE!! TURD OF A RAT!!! SEVEN YEARS A SLAVE!!! HAVE YOU NO SHAME?? HOW CAN YOU FACE ME NOW??

SAGE (his hand on his Ilm el-Ghaibat button in case he needs invisibility and teleportation): CALM YOURSELF! MAY ALLAH CALM YOU!

EGG (looks around in confusion): What? How?? Huh?!

SAGE (softly): Tell us what happened.

EGG (humbly,* with wonder, chants): I have been seven upon seven years a follower of Sidi Ahmed ben Yusuf of Miliana, who teaches the Prophet Mohammed could not have spoken with God ninety thousand times and still find the bed warm when he returned.
    My first seven years I spent in Sebou, devouring women.

---

*Subdued. Islam means "submission to God" and Muslim means "servant of God."

Seven times I have walked to Miliana, a gypsy of the desert, to visit the <u>marabout</u> of my false prophet.
My last seven years have I spent with my head in a jug of lilac water!
LA ILAHA IL'ALLAH OO M'HAMD URRASULULAH!!

He slowly turns and walks back, sitting crosslegged once more, facing Mecca. The CROWD disperses, murmuring.

This we saw personally. They say Rumi pulled this riff with Haroun el-Raschid and made an honest man out of him. Wood of lilac--to make lilac water--is available from any black desert "woman" selling herbs.
How do Americans relate to this scene? Well, the Moroccans don't deal with possession by industrial demons. Those who work with iron--blacksmiths, ironmongers, foreigners--are particularly despised in Marrakech. The Arabs invented lucky horseshoes.
They won't stone you unless you dress like a blacksmith. Dress like a foreign potentate and they'll fear some heavy curse. For Moroccans themselves, iron is <u>taboo</u>, except for magical purposes.
But didn't I say something about sporty new Fiats in the Casbah? That's a point, all right. We'll know for sure on the day of reckoning (the day the Jews cross the Jordan; the day of the California earthquake; the day the earth falls into the sun; January 1, 2000), but Arab odds makers are laying 777 to 1 that all Fiats and their owners are doomed. Going to be scorched earth?
Islam, incidentally, is the fastest growing religion in the world. With six hundred million fervent believers it now rivals Catholicism and China as the world's largest anything.
As a matter of fact, by the way, one of the storytellers in the Jamaa el-F'na now uses an amplifier and loudspeaker.

Makes a nice pile, too. I hear some big New York investors
are coming out to inspect his books, possible merger to ensue.

    Speaking of box office: Women's Liberation is a hot item
now. Where are the Arabs at on that one?
    Item: Most women wear veils. To foreigners they all look
exactly the same! All you see are their eyes, and sometimes
they're covered too! A real mind blower.
    Item: Women never go to cafes. All day long the cafes
and hash bars teem with dark and earnest men. The women stay
home or go to market.
    Item: Moslem men may have four wives. The Koran says,
" . . . as long as he can treat them equally." The king can
have as many as he wants; Mohammed had thirteen. If a man
commits adultery, pish and a few tushes. If a woman does it
she can be flogged.
    Item: Women can only own property when the moon is in
Taurus. They can refuse if a man wants to marry them, by law
if not custom. At a prewedding ceremony, local physiognomists
(called <u>qaif</u>) lift the prospective bride's veil for the first
time. They record her features to guard against future
substitution of an unmarried older sister. Peep-bo!
    Item: Men often hold hands here, and homosexuality is
completely accepted everywhere.
    I think the whole trip boils down to this: Arabs reproduce
to make more believers.

The Partridge, the Infant, and the Guest

A man, his wife and child lived off the fruits of the hunt. He hunted every day, and came home every night with three partridges: one for himself, one for his wife, and one for their son. He never brought back more than three.

But one day he brought back four.

As he came home, he found a stranger standing at his door. The man asked for hospitality.

"Welcome!" cried the hunter. "You are in luck today!" They went in.

His wife plucked the partridges, cleaned them, and threw them into the cooking pot. The hunter rose and said to the stranger, "Let us pray at the mosque, while we wait for our dinner." They went off.

Soon after, the child fell asleep at his mother's knee. The supper got cooked and the wife put out the fire, awaiting her husband and their guest. They were late, and she said to herself: "My son is asleep, he won't care. I'm hungry, so I'm going to eat his partridge as well as my own!" She ate both of them (they were delicious) and left the two others for her husband and their guest.

After a while she again said to herself: "I imagine our neighbors have offered to put up our guest, and they must surely have fed him!" So she ate his bird also. She left one for her husband, but when he still failed to show up she said to herself: "Well, no doubt he's gone to see his mother. It's foolish to wait for him any longer!" So she took his partridge and ate it too.

Soon the child woke up and began to cry. His mother didn't have anything more to feed him.

Meanwhile, the guest returned. He found the infant in tears and asked, "How come he's crying?"

She answered, "Well, usually when we have a guest we cut off his earlobes and give them to the child so he'll keep quiet!" When he heard this, the guest took off like a bat out of hell.

The husband came in just then and asked, "Why's he crying?"

"That guest of yours just fled with the partridges for our supper!" she exclaimed.

He shot off in pursuit. "Stop!" he cried, running. "Just leave a little piece for the child!"

Thinking he wanted a piece of his ear, the guest ran even faster, and yelled, "If you catch me, you're liable to cut off both of them!"

The vibes of Marrakech are red, green, and on a clear day, blue white. This is a heavy trip. Requires centering, penetration. The wit of a serpent and the spirit of a bird. The West at your back facing East is just exactly the opposite of the East at your back facing West.

Whereas at first blush the medina appears to foreigners as dusty crackabrain baked red walls and alleys, in reality it is lush lovely green gardens with a red herring grid fitted on. Blue-white comes from the mountains, the perishing Atlas. They lie to the East, as far as you can see. They separate Morocco from the mercury desert. Across the mighty Atlas at Zagora lies the apocryphal but true sign: "52 DAYS TO TIMBUCTOO."

At any given time, the Bedouins are sailing across the Sahara on their way to Marrakech for the festival of Ashoura. Or maybe they're on their way to Kairouan, in Tunisia, for a pilgrimage. Seven trips to Kairouan equals one to Mecca. Or maybe they're trying to make it to Mecca, or Samarkand, or Qandahar, or Rangoon. They're vitally involved in the high energy matrix on this planet.

Priorities. In order to blow away adversity you must put your--uh--Tao center to center with the--uh--Tao of the--uh--Universe.

The Bedouins and other high energy trippers are streaking

across Arabia because that's where they pick up on what's happening in the psychic world. Arab women are like that because that's tough Tao.

A paramagnet of the high-energy set, Marrakech attracts both poles. You get slaves of God and gods of slaves. "The Hashish Trail is a high energy scene where quickness of hand combined with slush fund of hard currency yields high profits. 'Invest in Morocco Energy Bonds!'"

Scene: The Sultan's Garden. We are naked. We sit in the lotus (half lotus in my case). East is duly faced. Meditations on far-distant galaxies. Arabian afternoon sun chessworks through blue branches. Suddenly:

BARBARA (whispering): Davie!

ME: Whuh?

BARBARA: Davie! There's a sound!

ME (coming down): What're you talking about?

BARBARA (going over to the south wall, toward our sandstone and rammed-earth shower): I heard something weird. (Her voice grows fainter with Doppler effect.)

A silence now as I try to pick up the broken vibes.

BARBARA (suddenly): DAVIE!!?

ME: What?!

BARBARA (shrieking): THERE'S A RAT IN THE BATHROOM!!

Fluid geography newsreel images flash onto north wall. New York: RATS CRAWL THROUGH TOILET BOWL, DEVOUR CHILDREN! Los Angeles: RATS AND BLACK WIDOWS ANNOUNCE SPRING OFFENSIVE! Calcutta: RATS AND BLACK FILTH SMEAR ASSHOLE OF THE WORLD! An endless loop of videotape horror upchucked from the slime of the deep.

ME (freaked-out scared): Oh. (Long pause.) Well. I'll come look. (Sure enough, there is a rat right in the fucking bathroom. Black beads fall from his eyes. Musical scales fall from mine, clattering atonally.) Uh. Let's go for a walk.

BARBARA: I agree.

We lock all the doors and put on some clothes lipperty-lip. Creak open the heavy front door. We have been blown right out of the sky by a psychic ack-ack.
    Street empty but for a fruitseller and some small children playing "Kikes and Gringoes." When the urchins see my head pop out of the door they rush over.

KIDS: Miss-yoor, miss-yoor, bon jour, miss-yoor, madame, miss-yoor, donne-moi l'argent, un dirham . . .

ME (in no mood to fuck around): Aiwa! Zit! Imshi! Ma andee hattashee! Wa-loo! Imshi!!

The KIDS are startled. They frown and mutter, then disperse.

ME: OK. Let's blow this joint.

We step into the street. An old man in a turban is walking his donkey. The fruitseller nods and we nod nervously back.
    We turn left around the corner, away from the fruit man. There is a thirty-foot wall on our left-- the other side of our bedroom wall--and small <u>baqal</u> on

the right: a bread baker, match-and-sundry shop, bits-and-pieces man, herbalist. Communal water tap. Community oven. We duck under a low archway. Three aged Arabs sit in its coolness, crosslegged, smoking and conversing in low tones. A tall woman hurries by, draped in a white robe from head to toe, nose and mouth veiled by a sheer slip of purple silk. A shopkeeper leers.

Farther down the street we turn into a tiny passage. All is suddenly quiet. This is residential Arabia. Standing in the center of the capillary, touching the cell walls on both sides with either elbow. We walk a little slower.

ME (still mind blown): A fucking rat!

BARBARA (together, as usual): Jesus!

ME (laughing nervously): Couple of middle-class pussies!

BARBARA: Yeah, but a rat's still not very groovy!

ME: Whether you like them or not!

BARBARA: So, Jesus. What are we going to do?

Well, well. We're confronted with an official U.S. Certified Bummer.

ME: Fuck if I know.

We shake our heads as we turn in front of the Dar Si Said museum. They run our lodgings, so we are quite chummy with a couple of their high-powered Islamic scholars. One of them doubles as caretaker in our Walled Garden, Arabian scholars not fearing to get their hands dirty. We spot him in the front hall of the museum.

ME: Hey, there's Brahim!

BARBARA: Should we tell him about the rat?

ME: Uh. He'll be over tomorrow. Let's tell him then.

We twist and turn. The medina has two trillion shortcuts. We instinctively head for the Jamaa el-F'na. It's the only place for a time like this. Meanwhile, it is dead quiet.
    The walls rise twenty feet on each side. A thin slash of sunlight penetrates. Now and then a small child--fingers orange with some leatherworking substance, open sores on head and hands--gives us a beaming smile. An Arab on a bicycle. A young girl balancing a plywood board on her head, thereon carrying two loaves of steaming round bread. Foreigners seldom go here.
    The narrow street winds into a small sunny plaza. Another communal well on the corner. Several children and young girls draw water in double pails. A rug MERCHANT sits outside his shop on a stool, reading the Koran. He looks up when he hears us coming, and immediately smiles. Pockets Koran.

MERCHANT: Hello. Please come and look inside.

ME: No thanks. Some other time. Bakee ma.

MERCHANT: Ah, you speak Arab. Mezyen bzef!

ME: Yeah, thanks. B'slamma.

MERCHANT (shrugs): B'slamma.

We hurry on. The street abruptly ends in another low archway, giving onto Riad Zitoun, one of the few named streets in the medina. It bustles like a motherfucker. Right turn.
    Though this is a main street, it is not more than ten feet wide. It is crammed with Arabs, Berbers, Bedouins, Kabyles, Germans, day trippers, musicians, small ass-pinching boys, pissing donkeys, bread ladies,

fruit men, soldiers, candlestick makers, untouchable ironmongers, Jews, black desert magicians, clangers, jostlers, hustlers, rustlers, doctors, scribes, lawyers, hashish eaters, and Swedish film crews. A French-made car insistently squeezes everyone up against the wall. It passes, only to be followed by a horse and carriage.

BARBARA: Fucking traffic!

ME: Yeah. Insane motherfuckers!

It was all convoluting. What had been quaint and exotic was becoming a bad trip. Thus turned inside out of the glove of change, we burst upon the Jamaa el-F'na!
    Cafe! Cafe! We lurch into the CTM. BOB and CORLENE, friends from the boat, are there.

BOB (tearing his gaze from a snake charmer): Hey, man, you look bughouse!

ME (breathless): Mind if we sit down?

CORLENE: Not atall. (She is 6'2".)

US: Thanks.

BOB: Hey, man, blah blah blah . . .

ME: We found a fucking rat in our place!

CORLENE: Ah hah hah hah . . .

BOB: A Rat!? Oh, wow!

ME: Yeah. What do you know about rats?

BOB: Hey, man, in New York City the rats come right out of the toilets and kill little children!

Just what we wanted to hear.

ME (frantic): Come on, man, what do you know about the little mothers?

BOB: No, man, I'm not bullshitting. In New York they have been known to crawl out of the toilets. Rats!

ME: Bull Shit! You fucking bullshitter!

BARBARA: Yeah, I went into the shower and there was this fucking rat staring right at me!

CORLENE: Oh, wow, man. I really don't dig rats.

ME: Yeah, Jesus Christ, me either!

BOB: Yeah, me either.

BARBARA: Me either.

That settles that.
    The Sultan's Palace, the next morning. We are up early, to make sure we get to BRAHIM before he's settled down on a leather pouf with a mint tea and a deck of ratty Arab cards.
    BRAHIM is old, about sixty, and a completely holy clean man. As I said, he's a far out Islamic scholar, attached to the museum. He cannot read; he knows the Koran by heart. Speaks French, Arabic, and Berber-Chleuh. We don't exactly know how he stands on rats.

ME: Good morning, Brahim! Ça va? (I extend my hand.)

BRAHIM (taking my hand briefly, then touching his heart and lips): Oui, ça va. Ça va?

ME (repeating the handshake ritual): Oui, oui. Ça va. Ça va bien. (This is a bloody lie.) Uh,

Brahim. Did you know there's a <u>rat</u> here? In the shower? A rat?

BRAHIM (calmly): Oui, oui. He lives in there.

ME (incredulous): He <u>lives</u> there??

BRAHIM: Yes. In the daytime he lives in the top of the trees. He steals the birds' eggs in order to stay alive.

ME: Crikey!!

CURTAIN falls, striking me a glancing blow between the eyes.

There it is. A material event with its logarithmically high-powered correlative in objective imagination. It was <u>essential</u> to fashion a new relationship of spirit to body and <u>body to</u> earth, else <u>blooey</u>! Unfocused psychic distress. FREAK OUT!!
    I leave it to some ultrahip Madison Avenue insurance company to write us a policy paying off on the dark side of the coin.
    How does one make it? Even as editor of a national magazine, owner of two houses and a Lear Jet, one wouldn't worry about where his exhaust fumes went. I mean he wouldn't <u>really</u> worry, not enough to get off the highways, grow his own <u>food,</u> and help himself to electricity from the wind. He might write an article about it, in Editorial Inveighings. Big fucking deal. We were confronted with a <u>rat</u>, motherfucker, right in our house! You don't just kill a <u>rat</u>, either. That's the whole thing. They could just as possibly kill you! I blush at my situation, born into a home where rats just didn't <u>go</u>.
    Well, I'll skip a few days of useless gloom. A Fact finally shot up straight and tall, shaking off all the clinging mutters:

The Rat lives here too. That is a no-bullshit, accept-what-befalls Fact! Changes had officially been gone through. (The straight community goes through channels; hippies go through changes.) Yes. That fucking Rat lived there too. That was all, genna-mun! We lived in the main room; the rat lived in the shower. Infuckingcredible!

Well. In brief, this began a complete psychic regeneration. We had Accepted. The Arab medina--Marrakech--was a Whole System. You took the quaint with the rats. You take the scientists with the atom bomb. If you live in the Middle Ages, you get the Middle Ages diseases.

Old World. New World.

Scene: Evening in the Atlas mountains. A HEDGEHOG meets a JACKAL.

HEDGEHOG: Where you going, man?

JACKAL: Seeking my fortune.

They go off together and eventually come upon a well. They are thirsty, so they want to drink. The HEDGEHOG jumps into one of the pulley-rigged pails and shoots down into the well. After drinking, he realizes he doesn't know how to get out again. He calls to the JACKAL.

HEDGEHOG: Hey, man, there's eight speckle-tit ewes down here with their little lambs! Quick, jump in the bucket!

The JACKAL jumps into the bucket and descends, raising the HEDGEHOG in the other bucket.

JACKAL (looks around): Hey man, what the fuck??

What is this shit, anyway?

HEDGEHOG: It's the changes of the low world, man. They raise some and drop others!

That story courtesy of the Tachelhit Berbers, Atlas mountain branch.

After this event, the hustlers left us alone. They knew. We were Initiates. I guess it shows in your aura. Working under false illusions creates a tissuepaper fortress around you. Any compass for fifteen miles goes haywire. And there's always someone kicking you in the ass, who disappears as soon as you turn around. Most tourists just blame it on the food.

But dig this: Although we had finally accepted Arabia, we knew that we were--more than ever--Westerners! The psychic eleven had pulled a double reverse with quarterback option. We induced. Reversed magnetic field.

Carl Jung once went into great detail proving that in each land there is a special relation of spirit to body and body to earth. When Europeans emigrate to America, their children's features become definitely more Indianized. Just something in the American soil. This is what really, psychically, makes a country, or a stamping ground.

Arabs obviously have a different spiritual relation to their environment than Americans to theirs. They have different polarity, or something. So to live in the Arab world one must change polarity, or else be battered about by ceaseless illusions. It is a matter of tuning in, just like with a radio set. Just a little off the beam and it's garble. Fine tuning, a little bandspread, and you're right on.

Very strange. Only at the point where we knew we weren't Arabian did the whole scene jell. The greatest safety lies in the heart of danger.

Scene: A JEW wants to take a shit one night. He is frightened to go out to the shitpile alone. He speaks to his WIFE.

JEW: Come with me!

WIFE: But, man, there's nothing to be afraid of! Go on!

But he won't listen; she finally goes with him. He squats at the shitpile and sees the moon shining brilliantly overhead.

JEW: Ah, the moon! How it glistens! It guides the holy storks flying to far-off Doukkala!

He is four days from Doukkala--present-day Marrakech. His WIFE says to him:

WIFE: Shut up, Mouchi! You didn't even have the courage to come out to the shitpile alone and now you talk to me about the land of Doukkala!

Survivors of the shitwreck of Identity clambering over the brink. Dedalus and Icarus passing out waterwings.

Had the habit of commandeering a rooftop on the Jamaa el-F'na, in the interest of overview. Would contemplate the swirling virus below while sipping mint tea and dismembering <u>Herald Tribune</u>. I quote from my notebook:

    EXCITEMENT!! Slow day, right after "Trône," the festival of Piggery. Only one set each of snake charmers, witches and winnowing fans.
    Nervous sigh of relief with morning coffee and American Daily Blatt. Some infiltrator dude injecting pig disease into Canadian bloodstream--runs for cover into USA . . . Spain and Morocco swapping pirate coves for left-wingers . . . pal to Presidents sick and tired of uppity niggers, calls for some benign malevolence. . . .
    Many friends splitting today for quiet seaside fishing towns, Tunisia and Europe. City scene gets to you, Marrakech or N.Y.
    After all, if we had wanted diversion and action we could have stayed in Berkeley. We want ENLIGHTENMENT, by God, and we'll pay good American dollars to get it!

    From a heuristic, touristic bias, Marrakech is hub of some far out freakies. Due west on the Atlantic is Essaouira, the magic capital of the Maghreb. Due east is Beni Mellal, an important Berber city. Farther east lies Zagora, right on the fringe of the Sahara. Southward sits the Spanish Sahara, the free port at Tantan, and the camel market of Goulimine.
    But the Jamaa el-F'na is renowned throughout Africa as <u>the</u> scene for certified mindblowing. Marrakech the Red.

Scene: Marrakech Express, second-class compartment. Lot has thrown us together with an agent of the political police.

ENQUIRING REPORTER: And just what kind of things do you investigate?

ABDUL, BADGE NO. 33: Oh, you know, there are always some--a small minority, I assure you--who commit crimes against the King!

REPORTER: You live in Marrakech?

ABDUL PIG: No, in Rabat.

REPORTER: Ah.

The train rumbles on: "upchuckit upchuckit upchuckit upchuckit upchuckit upchuckit upchuckit upchuckit. . . ."

REPORTER: And now you're going to Marrakech?

ABDUL PIG: Yes. First to Marrakech, then to Tizi n'Tichka. (This is a town in the mountains, near the legendary Ourika Valley.)

REPORTER: Ah.

"upchuckit upchuckit upchuckit upchuckit upchuckit. . . ."

REPORTER: You travel quite a bit then?

ABDUL PIG (smiles): Ah, no. I have never been out of Morocco.

REPORTER (mentally crossing out border dispute with Algeria): Ah.

"upchuckit upchuckit upchuckit upchuckit upchuckit. . . ."

REPORTER: Say, could you tell me something about those

student demonstrations we've heard about? What're they all about, anyway?

ABDUL PIG: Ahh, just the Communists and the Jews. Nothing serious. It'll all be over soon.

Though tough, Morocco is not any fascist dogdom like the USA. So our ENQUIRING REPORTER asks:

REPORTER: But, ah, the capitalists and the Christians? They're not exactly the jewels in the lotus, are they?

ABDUL PIG: Look, I'm just doing my job, gotta wife and kids, y'see . . .

REPORTER: Um.

"upchuckit upchuckit"

REPORTER: What about kif? Busted anyone for kif?

ABDUL PIG: Oh, yes. Ketama is the center for kif and hashish. I have been there (smiling) many times. Many Moroccans get caught for kif. It is against the law, you know.

REPORTER: I know. So where do you fit into the cosmic scheme of things?

ABDUL PIG: I am a servant of the King, and of Allah.

"upchuckit"

The word is that some Berber tribes, based in and around Tizi n'Tichka, are carrying on a longtime blood-revolution against the "Arab" administration. Since most Moroccans have both Arab and Berber blood it is hard to recruit new guerrillas, but the Berbers have a vibe called sof that binds a tribe like glue. The tribes behind the fighting in Ifni, Spanish Sahara, and Algeria are all ancient Berber clans that have opposed foreign invasions since the (gulp!) beginning of time. No written language, you understand, so no one knows anything for sure except those old, wrinkled Berber chieftains.

Remember how we learned in World History about the Dark Ages? No one had it together, bubonic plague, Europe in a tizzy, just absolutely nothing happening at all . . . now we'll study Christianity. Well, that is a bunch of bullshit! While Europe was wallowing in its ignorance, the Arabs (those dirty little guttersnipes) had the greatest civilization known to man! In fact, they say the gross national product of the Baghdad regime exceeded the present GNP of the United States! Baghdad held sway from Spain to Malaya. Talk about power! The fundamental discoveries of modern medicine were made by Arabs! The university at Fez, in Morocco, is the oldest in existence! And I'm sure you've heard of Arabic numbers. OK. At the pinnacle of this power there were two clefts in the outthrust Arab chin: the Near East and North Africa. Baghdad and Marrakech. Persians and Moors. The Caliphate of Haroun el-Raschid and the Bahia Palace.

It got to be just about a toss-up which capital of the Arab world was the more exotic: Baghdad with its delicate, intricate counterplots or Marrakech with its African blowpipes.

Who is responsible for this fabulous empire in northwest Africa? The Berbers, that's who! Our old pals. The heathen savages. Just as soon roast your head as look at you. That's who!

Earlier we spoke of the Arabs and the Berbers--how the Berbers by and large accepted Islam and carried on. The mixture of Arab and Berber made the Moor. It was a Berber chieftain, converted to Islam, who built the Moorish empire of West Africa and Spain. Here flourished some of the heaviest heads in the whole cosmos. Ibn el-Arabi, author of The Alchemy Of Happiness and one of the most revered Sufis ever. Dahiya, the Jewish Berber Queen of Ifriqiya. Yusuf of Andalusia. (Yes, incidentally, there are many Jewish Berber tribes! Interesting, ain't it? What's more, the only linguist hip enough to crack Berber languages is astonished yes astonished that they are similar to ancient Egyptian Coptic.) Marrakech--the locus of the great Moorish civilization.

Basically, the Berber-Moorish empire flourished. The Jews

and Arabs got along famously for several hundred years, land was held rent-free and the incredibly rich region prospered. Then, just like the jackal and the hedgehog, the Caliph of Baghdad--Haroun el-Raschid--got sticky fingers. He sent one of his wazirs out to Marrakech to see what was what. Posing as a survey taker, he wormed his way into the royal court. They had tea. The Wazir said that actually he was checking advertising penetration out here in the hinterlands, looking for royal families (". . . like yourselves . . .") he could entrust with the Sacred Books. When they flashed he was just selling encyclopedias, the Moors threw him out. But the damage had been done. The Wazir had uncorked a small vial of clear liquid into the tea. Two days later the Moorish king was dead.

    A court of inquiry said it was just the work of the lone encyclopedia salesman. They discounted any conspiracy, but the Empire began to disintegrate.

    Scene: Outside the walls of Marrakech. Sky a bitter blue, walls long and low and salmon red, mosques and turrets etched on the backdrop. Ramparts. Thrill. Thousands milling about like black ants pincered by the slavemakers. They crawl everywhere except inside a magic circle described by a Berber chieftain's circus-type tent in the center. The circle measures two thousand years in diameter.

    One hundred and eight Berber horsemen sit righteously astride one hundred and eight snorting black Arabian stallions. They wear black turbans and flowing white <u>burnous</u>. Each shoulders his piece: a seven-foot muzzleloader with inlaid mother-of-pearl handle. They line up facing east, along the diameter of the circle. Their blinding clarity rings in the bright sunlight.

    Inside the tent: richly carpeted ground, low cushions, subtle incense from Kairouan. The Berber sheikh sits crosslegged, in the American Indian rather than the Yoga manner. He sips herbal tea.

As he puts down his glass and begins to meditate an electric circuit is completed. Without warning the ferocious horsemen charge on the crowd at full gallop! Muskets skyward they fire tremendous booming volleys! Only fifty yards from the crowd! Full gallop, full gallop! BOOM! BOOM! One hundred and eight murderous Berbers, madmen with rifles, savage, wicked, evil Berbers!! Charging the crowd, full gallop! Twenty yards! Horses frothing, Berbers shouting, charging. Full gallop! BOOM!! Full gallop!! THEY'RE CHARGING THE CROWD! THEY'RE ON TOP OF THE CROWD!! Just at the last possible microsecond: dead stop!

The crowd's adrenalin is up to about a googolplex! The echo of musket fire, the swirling dust from hoofbeats! Cosmic yab!

This is the <u>Fantasía</u>. We saw it on the festival of Trône, when the king runs down his good deeds to the people.

Scene: A narrow, busy street in the medina in Marrakech. It is twilight. Everyone scurries. The muezzin wails out his call to prayer. Foot and futuristic traffic. We happen to fall into step with an OLD MAN wearing a plain wool djellaba, a white turban, and yellow leather curled toe slippers. Shuffling at a very easy pace, he is rhythmically whacking his donkey every few steps.

OLD MAN (in translation): How do, friend!

ME: How are you? No problems? No bad scenes?

OLD MAN: Nope, everything's cool. Any bad scenes with you?

ME: No, not with me either, friend. (We shake hands and touch our hearts.) Well. What are you up to?

OLD MAN: Oh, same as always. (Whacks his donkey.) This here's my donkey.

ME: Nice donkey.

OLD MAN: Thanks. She's all I have.

ME: All you have?

OLD MAN: Yep. She's my house, my wife, my auto, my keep, and of course my donkey!

ME: Wow. (Mulling it over.) Uh, could you do with any spare change?

OLD MAN (hesitates): Do you have more?

ME: Yeah, sure, here, take it! (Trying to hand him coins.)

OLD MAN: Well, wait a minute. Do you want to make more, or do you expect more? Even more?

ME: Yes. Look, here, take it!

OLD MAN: Then you keep it. You need it more than I do. You have much and want more; I have nothing and want nothing.

Whacks his donkey as we part at a crossroads.

Was this Khidr the Jew, the Green One? Possibly. He is often diffused among the people. We once saw him passed around by ten J'lallah dancers, whirling dervishes of the Maghribi school, on Mohammed's birthday. But then, that was a festival day, and there's no telling what may happen.

Scene: Eve of Ashoura, the tenth day of the New Year. You can only buy chickpeas at the market, you must not strike the ground with a stick, you may not shave, get married, or cut your nails. This means YOU! We sit in the Walled Garden, woolgathering.

BARBARA: Man, they're acting weird today!

ME: Yeah, I noticed it too. I think it's this holiday, Ashoura.

BARBARA: What's it all about?

ME: I dunno, exactly. "Ashra" means "ten" in Arabic. Brahim said it's something to do with the burning bush, but I don't really know.

At this point we lapse into silence. A dull, insistent drumming penetrates consciousness and we realize it has been going on for quite a while.

ME: Hear those drums?

BARBARA: Yeah.

The drumming gets louder.

ME: The natives are actually fucking <u>restless</u> tonight! Wow! (We laugh.)

BARBARA: Let's go see what's happening.

We open the heavy door and look both ways. The fruitseller has closed up shop. The street is deserted, but the drumming is quite close now, insistent, an endless quick dah-duh-duh-dah-duh-duh dah-duh-duh-dah-duh-duh . . .)
We step into the street, unassailed for once. We turn the corner and get the shock of our not uneventful lives! The street is packed and everyone is masked! We identify a wolf, a lion, a camel. Some people are not masked, but dressed very weirdly.
Center stage we see six Berbers: two dressed as LIONS, one YOUNG GIRL, her husband, one BAILIFF, and one OLD MAN with a huge white beard, the bottom half dyed red, wearing a hat made of snail shells and a cape of porcupine quills!
The OLD MAN is speaking, and the drumming subsides to a low punctuation. He is a PROPHET, it appears, and has just returned from Mecca. He pronounces predictions for the CROWD, which seem to be inside jokes of some sort. Then the others form a tribunal. The PROPHET speaks:

PROPHET: I come from Mecca! I haven't gone far, since I just left this morning.

FIRST LION: So what's new in Mecca?

PROPHET: Grain is very cheap.

SECOND LION: How much for eight double decaliters?

PROPHET: One hundred five francs.

YOUNG GIRL: That's very expensive!

PROPHET: Since you did not even go, it cost you nothing! Me, I pray God the price stays the same!

Fires suddenly ignite in smudge pots in the street. Incense is thrown on freely. The drumming turns up. A

dark man in an orange turban plays a buzz-flute. Everyone
has a drum made from fired clay with a stretched goatskin.
On cue the drumming subsides and the PROPHET speaks
once more.

PROPHET (indicating the young girl): Who is this slut?
  Who is she?

CROWD: She is Kahina, wife of Ahmed.

PROPHET: Humbug! You are duped by the women who
  blow on knots!

CROWD: What? How? What is this? Kif?

YOUNG GIRL: I--I . . .

CROWD: Silence!!

PROPHET (chanting):   One hundred years ago
                      This fair-haired girl
                      With her beauty mark
                      Bewitched my one and only son.

                      Now, after their long separation,
                      My son sends me to say
                      He loves her still
                      And besides, he now has saved up
                      Some good karma!

The tribunal deliberates. The CROWD bets on the
outcome. Drums roll for suspense.

BAILIFF: We decide . . . that this girl be restored
  to her first husband. That is our judgment, and
  we welcome the springtime!

The music resumes once more. The CROWD dances a frenzy.
Everyone makes an offering, and the fires lick the
silent walls.

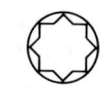

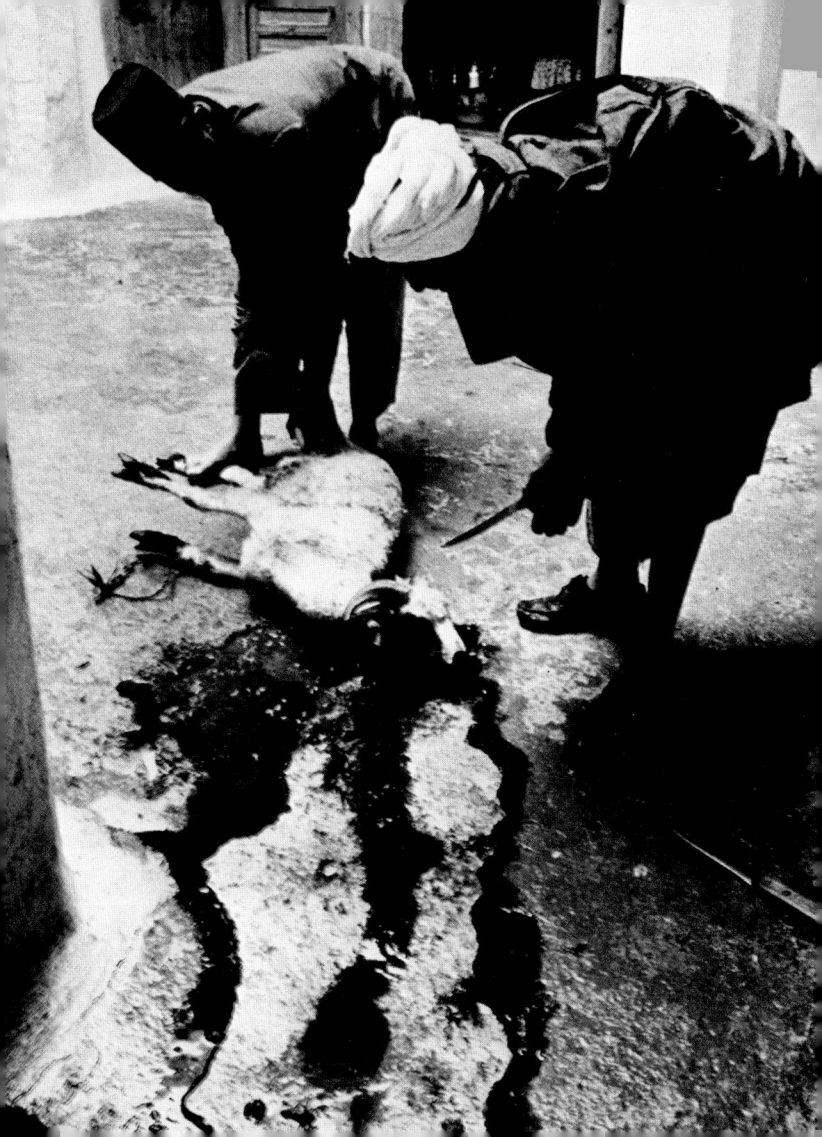

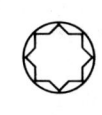

Compare this kind of ritual murder with the one where the Chief of Staff picks a name "at random" to be killed in Indochina.

As you see, by now our B.A.s were wearing off. Here was a fantastix culture, the Moors, that we sure hadn't learned about at mother's knee. All our income tax deductions changed into intuitions. We told time by the heavens, not by mechanical pointers.

And what is the payoff? How does this relate to AmeriKKKa? It would take a heavy charm to change Armoricans into peace-loving Arabs--something like a black cloud over New York or a blight on the drinking water. As far as Marx goes, the medina is just another feudal economy. Its evolution to capitalism is plain as the soot on your face. But in cold, hard, magical terms. . . .

Morocco has been around for ten thousand years. The USA is just a newborn babe, or one of those aggressive, awkward adolescents. Changes only occur according to the capacity of the experiencer.

Jafar, the son of Yahya of Lisbon, determined to find the Sufi "Teacher of the Age," and he traveled to Mecca as a young man to seek him. There he met a mysterious stranger, a man in a green robe, who said to him before any word had been spoken:

"You seek the Greatest Sheikh, the Teacher of the Age. But you seek him in the East, when he is in the West. And there is another thing which is incorrect in your seeking."

He sent Jafar back to Andalusia, to find the man he named--Mohiuddin, son of el-Arabi, of the tribe of Hatim-Tai. "He is the Greatest Sheikh."

Telling nobody why he sought him, Jafar found the Tai family in Murcia and inquired for their son. He found that he had actually been in Lisbon when Jafar set off on his travels. Finally he traced him to Seville.

"There," said a cleric, "is Mohiuddin." He pointed to a mere schoolboy, carrying a book on the Traditions, who was at that moment hurrying from a lecture hall.

Jafar was confused, but stopped the boy and said, "Who is the Greatest Teacher?"

"I need time to answer that question," said the other.

"Art thou the only Mohiuddin, son of el-Arabi, of the tribe of Tai?" asked Jafar.

"I am he."

"Then I have no need of thee."

Thirty years later in Aleppo, he found himself entering the lecture hall of the Greatest Sheikh, Mohiuddin ibn el-Arabi, of the tribe of Tai. Mohiuddin saw him as he entered, and spoke:

"Now that I am ready to answer the question you put to me, there is no need to put it at all. Thirty years ago, Jafar, thou hadst no need of me. Hast thou still no need of me? The Green One spoke of something wrong in thy seeking. It was time and place."

Jafar, son of Yahya, became one of the foremost disciples of el-Arabi.

--Idries Shah, <u>The Way of the Sufi</u>

IV

IN WHICH WE CONSULT THE MYTHS OF FREE MEN

    No one can fool the Ait Sadden. They're the canniest motherfuckers this side of the Ganges. Have you forgotten that even Satan himself couldn't fuddle them? In fact, <u>they</u> diddled <u>him</u>! Why, my great-grandfather told me t<u>hat</u> at the t<u>ime</u> of Creation Satan and only Satan had any fire. (We all know he's got fire, right?) Well, one of the Ait Sadden went down to Hell to take a look at it--maybe to buy it off him. Just in case, he took along the stalk of a giant fennel. Never can tell, especially with Satan.
    Well, of course, the Prince of the Dark was surprised to see him, and our ancestor got right to the point.
    "How much you want for fire, Satan?" he asked.
    "Fuck off, Berber dog!" Satan answered snappily. He knew where his account was kept.
    As the Ait Sadden wheedled, "Aw, come on, Satan, be a sport for once!" he began to unobtrusively swish his stalk around.

"Beat it, creep, or you'll be in here permanently!" menaced Satan.

Suddenly the Berber hauled ass out of there! swishing his ferrule like mad and screaming:

"OK, asshole, fuck you, fuck you, I'm not buying!!"
And his tinder stalk caught fire, which he brought back to the world of men, booty from the Devil!

Frankly, the Berbers don't believe American astronauts flew to the moon. Lot of shit. Some crazy hype. They know, because they've been up there for--oh, say--twenty thousand years! Telepathic contact. Much less messy than dropping eight pounds of radioactive plutonium into the sea. Shit, if you can discover fire you can surely make telepathic contact with the moon. Easier, in fact. The Tarot was invented in Morocco.

Scene: Berber village. Cock-crow. The WOMEN grind barley.

WOMEN (chanting):   Bismillah rrahman urahim
                    Bismillah nzwar d-ubbi. . . .

They have previously primed the mill with salt, which gives the blessing--baraka. By "mill" understand a neolithic flat stone anchoring a pivoting smaller stone. Each day, after grinding, the mill must be fed. A bit of grain is left in its eye.

A tall, proud, sinewy MAN comes in, wearing a turban twisted out of rough muslin and a thickish cream burlap djellaba. His face is thin--a scraggly beard grows-- but deeply, deeply tanned and lined. He chews a strand of mountain herb.

MAN (frowning): Hustle, hustle, women! The <u>moqaddem</u> is waiting; he grows impatient!

WOMEN (chanting): Bismillah rrahman urahim
                    Bismillah nzwar d-ubbi. . . .

We leave the WOMEN and make our way along the mud walls into a sunny little square. A circle of smooth stones marks the village threshing floor; today it is covered with rich red carpets, hand embroidered with the strange symbols that veil the history of the Berber race. The <u>moqaddem</u>--the sheikh--sits in a chair next to a man with a three-finger drum. They both wear white turbans and robes. The <u>moqaddem</u> sports a necktie underneath.

    The other tribesmen sit crosslegged on the ground. Some of their WOMEN are grinding the grain, others sit in the magic circle bedecked in white caftans with green sashes, wearing necklaces of semiprecious stones big as a big toe and headdresses of scarlet cords hung with clusters of silver and gold disks. The WOMEN have face tattoos which mark them as Haodéguines: large black spots at the outer corners of the eyes, smaller spots two inches below on the cheekbones, and a line running from chin to lower lip, intersected by five small parallel lines. Before them lie tambourines and teapots--the accouterments of the Berber race.

    Seven young girls pose backbent in the center of the circle, their legs tucked underneath, heads touching the carpet. They are motionless. They wear plain but elegant white robes, sashed, and green headbands. Their hair is knotted into 108 tiny, tiny braids.

    The grinding WOMEN appear, solemnly, carrying the season's first offering in a red ceramic bowl. They sprinkle it over the motionless girls and immediately the drums and tambourines activate! Six WOMEN with tambourines divide into two chorus lines, and sing responsively.

FIRST LINE: My heart is smitten with the son of Sidi Daoud! Why does he not look at me?

SECOND LINE: Because he was accompanied by his father!

FIRST LINE: Her heart is smitten with the son of Sidi Daoud! Who will say why he had not looked at her?

SECOND LINE: Because a wasp made him a nose like a fist!

FIRST LINE: O, her poor heart, it is taken by the son of Sidi Daoud! Why does he ignore her?

SECOND LINE: Because he has just been carrying manure!

The song continues for hours; the young girls in the center dance out the verses. When the song is over and the young girls exhausted, they are led into a small tent in which dozens of oil lanterns flame. There they meet their mothers. They are to be tattooed.

TATTOOED BERBER (casually): Ah, yes. Whoever is tattooed will perish in Hell. It is written.

The mothers prepare the tattooing inks: secret herbs. The girls lie down on mats, too exhausted to mind the stinging pain which initiates them into the dynasty of Sidi Ali bin Nasr. The tattoos are the only remnants of a language once written. Nowadays, the Berbers have no need for writing.
   When the ceremony is over, each girl has a blue sun with seven rays on her chin. An "X" nestles in the cleft with a line rising from the vertex of the "X" straight up through the lower lip. Three small spots over each eyebrow. This is a tradition that predates the pharaohs of Egypt.
   The eldest MOTHER tells the seven girls the following tale.

MOTHER: A man had seven wives. They were all sterile. He sought out a very old man and declared to him, "Sidi, I have married seven women and they are sterile!"

"Give them" he said, "some woolens to wash. Then throw some apricots into the current, upstream from where they are washing. Whoever catches an apricot will bear you a child!"

This was done. Each wife bore a child every time she caught an apricot. One of them caught only one fruit, and she had only one child. His name was Wargemas.

When the boys were growing up, the proud father bought them each a horse. He gathered them all and said: "My sons, I wish to see you perform the fantasía! A true son of mine will be able to snatch this gold plate off the ground while standing on his galloping horse!" The brothers went off together, but Wargemas galloped away by himself and plucked the plate off the ground!

From that moment, his brothers despised him.

Some time later they drew lots to see who would take the horses out to pasture. Wargemas was chosen. He began to cry. His mother, also crying, made him some excellent provisions. His father's other wives filled his rucksack with dried dung, which he thought was bread.

When he had gone out to pasture and had finally finished his mother's food, he turned to his rucksack. Inside he only found withered dung. He began to cry. A raven, passing by, exclaimed: "What is it, O pleasant face that tears should not sadden?"

"Oh, my dear bird, what will become of me? Oh, woe is me!"

"Don't worry! Be happy! Just take your horses over to that mosque, and when night falls go inside. There someone will bring you food. But a warning: Whatever you do, do not break the bone you will find there!"

Wargemas did as the raven suggested. He was quite content for some days. But one day his mind had engineered the exact situation for him and he said to himself, "By Allah, I must break that bone!" He ate his fill, then broke the bone.

Immediately, the mosque door swung shut. He was

locked in. He could find no exit. His horses waited for him outside. Wargemas sat down and cried.

The raven flew in and asked, "Why do you cry now, O fair one whom tears should not sully?"

"Oh, raven, I did not heed you and I broke the bone! And now the door has shut on me!" he wailed. The raven pitied him and went to open the door. He even led Wargemas's horses down to the stream to drink. But when he returned, Wargemas was still crying.

"Why do you still weep, O fair one whom tears should not visit?"

"Because I've taken the horses out to pasture, but when I return my brothers are only going to give me the worst nag of the whole lot!"

"Don't worry! Be happy! Just go now and water your horses. I will fly above their heads and only the noblest among them will raise his head from the water to look at me. To this one, stick a needle in his knee and a coin in his eye. Your brothers will tell you that since you blinded and lamed him, only you can ride him!"

This was done. When Wargemas returned, his brothers said: "This horse is blind and he's got a broken leg. No one but you will ride him!"

Hearing this, his mother broke into tears. "Leave him alone," she cried. "My son has had all the worry and responsibility of taking the horses to pasture and now you want to give him one that is lame and blind!" But Wargemas consoled her and said, "Don't cry, mother. I accept the judgment of my brothers. Whichever they wish to give me, I will take!"

That night, he heated some water, took some bran, and rubbed the horse down until he was groaning with pleasure. He removed the needle and the coin, and his horse was the noblest and most beautiful of all.

One day, months later, the father said to his gathered sons, "A true son of mine will bring me a bird from Saghozlan!"

They took off for the hunt and Wargemas happened to find one of these rare creatures. Returning from the hunt, the brothers met at a well by the foot of a mountain, upstream from the road.

"Did anyone find one of those damned birds?" they grumbled.

"I did!" answered Wargemas brightly.

Then and there, his brothers wanted to kill him.

"Give him a chance," one of them said mercifully.

"No, kill him!" shouted another.

"Throw him into the well!" insisted a third. This sounded right. They seized him and threw him into the well. He disappeared into the black water and sank so deeply his skin stripped off and rose to the surface.

Later a wandering troubadour came to the well to quench his thirst. He found the floating skin. He stretched it onto a gourd, improvising a drum, and thus continued to wander from land to land.

Whenever he would strike his new drum, the skin spoke: "Adah! Adah! O, troubadour, my brother killed me for a bird of Saghozlan!"

The troubadour wandered from Inja to Anja, crossing many countries, making a nice pile by virtue of his remarkable instrument. At last, he arrived in the region where Wargemas's sister now lived. He beat on the drum and the skin spoke: "Adah! Adah! O, troubadour, my brother killed me for a bird of Saghozlan!"

The girl cried out: "By Allah! O, _meddah_, let me try that drum!"

The troubadour obliged and the girl struck the drumhead. "Adah! Adah! O, sister, our brother killed me for a bird of Saghozlan!" The young girl burst into tears and said, "It's my brother!"

She went off to find her father. They returned together and she showed him the speaking drum. The father took it and beat on it.

"Adah! Adah! O, father, my brother killed me for a bird of Saghozlan!"

The father wept, wept so much that he couldn't see anymore. He took the drum home to his other sons, the ones who had thrown Wargemas into the well. He handed the drum to one of them, who struck it.

"Adah! Adah! O, brother, my brother killed me for a bird of Saghozlan!"

Then another took it, and another, and finally the drum reached the hands of the one who had actually thrown him in the well.

"Adah! Adah! O traitor! You killed me for a bird of Saghozlan!"

The grieving father built a pyre and burned his six sons. He kept the speaking drum and paid what he could afford to the troubadour.

The eldest MOTHER waves her hand. A Persian curtain drops and we see no more. The next morning the girls are married.

Well, I don't propose to be scholarly about the Berbers. No one is. Most chroniclers dismiss them as barbarians. That's where the name "Berber" comes from. I may not be an anthropologist, but I know what I like.

The Berbers are about the most together people anywhere. They are so anarchistic they have never formed a unified Berber nation (except for one brief period) in their entire history. Tribes ally to repel the common enemy, then go back to the land.

They pay dues for their anarchy. Even though they descend from fabulous Egypt, and even though they shared in the salad days of Islam, they have voluntarily chosen to live primitive and simple. They make their huts from mud, though their ancestors made them from gold. They cook on hot tiles, though their neighbors in the cities use bottled gas.

The French Foreign Legion tried to make the Berbers into a tasty bicot, but found their bark as hard as the cedars rooted in the high Atlas. So the European chefs changed frying pans and oiled the history books, claiming "a successful Berber sauce" in 1933. But when the French quit Morocco in 1952, to bloodier crush some Kabyle Berbers in Algeria, it was because they swooned at the hardihood of Morocco's mountain tribes.

By being anarchists the Berbers had foiled defeat: there was no one authorized to surrender! The perfect guerrilla government.

Scene: Night in the Berber capital. Apex of the Golden Age. The new Sultan has just succeeded to the throne. He finds himself unable to sleep.

SULTAN: Strange! By Allah, I sense something is afoot somewhere in my realm!

He gets up and dresses in the garb of a poor man. He leaves the palace by a secret exit and makes his way out into the cool air of his purple night capital. He has not gone far when he hears some whispering. He follows the sound and nearly falls over three MEN in turbans sitting under a small Moorish archway, smoking.

SULTAN: Greetings! May Allah bless you with peace!

MEN: Peace be with you, O stranger!

SULTAN (friendly): Allah willing, might I know what you three are doing here at this hour of the night?

MEN: We're waiting!

SULTAN: Ah. And if it please Allah, might I inquire who you are?

MEN: Why, we're the gazelles of the night! And who might _you_ be, O stranger who asks many questions?

SULTAN: I too am a gazelle of the night!

MEN: Praise Allah! (They all shake hands.)

SULTAN (to the FIRST MAN): You, my friend! In what manner does Allah favor you?

FIRST MAN: Ah, praise Allah. When a dog barks I know what he says!

SULTAN: Remarkable! (To SECOND MAN.) And you, O worthy friend? How has our Lord Allah gifted you?

SECOND MAN: Allah willing, I can tell what is happening on the other side of a wall!

SULTAN: Extraordinary! (To THIRD MAN.) And what about you, my friend?

THIRD MAN: Praise the Lord, I can knock a hole in a wall and fix it up again without leaving any trace!

SULTAN: Amazing! What amazing gazelles!

MEN: And what about you, O curious friend? What is your métier?

SULTAN: Why, I can dry up the vital juices in the mouths of men!

MEN: Ah! Your gift is likewise extraordinary!

SULTAN: And so, my new friends, where shall we go now? What shall we do?

MEN: Come with us! We're going to rob the Sultan!

They all arise and set off in the direction of the Royal Palace: the three GAZELLES and the disguised SULTAN. Along the way they meet a dog, who barks at them insistently.

GAZELLE: Where is he who understands the barking of dogs?

GAZELLE: Right here!

GAZELLE: What did he say?

GAZELLE: He says the Sultan is among us!

SULTAN: Ridiculous! The Sultan is asleep in his palace! What does a lowly dog know?

They kick the animal. Soon they arrive at the palace walls.

GAZELLE: Where is he who sniffs behind a wall?

GAZELLE: Right here!

GAZELLE: What is on the other side of this wall?

GAZELLE: It's a roomful of Negresses!

They skulk farther along the wall.

GAZELLE: What's behind the wall here?

GAZELLE: It's the kitchen!

They continue farther.

GAZELLE: What about here?

GAZELLE: Aha. This is the Sultan's bedroom.

GAZELLE: Is the Sultan inside?

GAZELLE: No, he's not!

SULTAN: Undoubtedly he went off to pray!

They continue.

GAZELLE: And what about here?

GAZELLE: Here is the Treasure Chamber!

Without a word, the penetrator of walls goes to it. When he finishes, he addresses the SULTAN.

GAZELLE (to SULTAN): Enter!

The SULTAN personally enters the Treasure Chamber and brings back a sack full of jewels.

GAZELLES: Go back for more!!

The SULTAN brings out another, then another, and a fourth. Each has his own sack, the SULTAN as well as the others. They ask the wallbreaker to fix up the wall. This done, they split. Each one carries his own sack. They find them extremely heavy and stop to rest.

GAZELLES (to SULTAN): OK, now, stranger, take your cut and beat it! Imshi!

SULTAN: But I could never keep so much for myself!

GAZELLES: What do you mean, O strange stranger?

SULTAN: I am afraid to take away so much gold. Tomorrow, at daybreak, when I go down to the souk to buy clothes and silk, people will surely be curious about where I got all this money!

GAZELLES: So what?

SULTAN: You see, never before did I even possess one sou. It would be very unusual. . . . Look. You take my sack. When I need anything I'll come and ask you for it! (He gives over his sack to one of the GAZELLES.)

GAZELLES: All right. OK. Go now, and God be with you. Whenever you need anything, simply come to us!

The SULTAN takes leave. He walks a few steps, then suddenly stops and turns around.

SULTAN: I have just realized that I don't know who you all are! Tomorrow, to find you again, whom shall I look for?

GAZELLES: What? You don't know who we are?

SULTAN: No.

GAZELLE ONE: I am the muezzin!

GAZELLE TWO: I am the imam!

GAZELLE THREE: And I am the clerk!

SULTAN: May Allah then keep you in holy peace!

The SULTAN returns to the palace by a roundabout route. He sleeps quite soundly until morning. At the appointed hour the next morning, he goes down to the mechouar, where he holds his audiences. He calls together his council of advisors, and whispers into his GRAND VIZIR'S ear.)

SULTAN (whispering): At noon, you will go to the mosque and station yourself in the front row of worshipers. After prayers, quietly ask the muezzin, the imam and the clerk to come and see me!

This is done.

MUEZZIN (upset, to IMAM): What does the Sultan want with us?

IMAM: Calm yourself. He undoubtedly just wants to talk to us. He's the new Sultan; he probably wants to ask us about our work at the mosque!

The VIZIR accompanies them to the palace and shows them

into an antechamber, where they spend the night. The next morning, the SULTAN asks the VIZIR where they are.

VIZIR: In the next room, where they can hear you.

SULTAN: Send in the first.

The VIZIR leads in the MUEZZIN.

SULTAN: Sit down. What is your position?

MUEZZIN: Your Majesty, I am the muezzin of the mosque. I rise in the middle of the night to praise God and to call the Muslims to prayer!

SULTAN: Yes, of course. But that's not what I mean!

MUEZZIN: I do not understand Your Majesty.

SULTAN: I would know what _else_ you do during the night!

Hearing this from the SULTAN's lips, the MUEZZIN's saliva dries up. He speaks thickly.

MUEZZIN: Majesty . . . when a dog barks, I know what he says!

SULTAN: Perfect! That's just what I wanted to know! (To VIZIR.) Put him into another room and send in the next.

This is done.

SULTAN (to IMAM): I would know, what is your métier?

IMAM: Majesty, I am imam of the mosque. I direct the prayers of Muslims, making sure they don't miss a propitious moment!

SULTAN: There is no question about that, of course. But I wish to know your--outside interests.

IMAM: Excellency, I have the ability to tell what is on the other side of a wall!

SULTAN: Excellent! Just what I wanted to know!

The VIZIR takes him off to keep the MUEZZIN company, and leads in the CLERK.

SULTAN: Please inform me as to what you can do.

CLERK: O Noble Sultan, Commander of the Faithful, I read the traditions from the sacred books and explain to the Faithful the words of God and His Prophet!

SULTAN: Yes, of course . . . but what do you do that is out of the ordinary?

CLERK (thickly): Effendi . . . I can pierce a wall and then repair it again perfectly!

SULTAN: Just so. Take him away also!

The inquisition over, the SULTAN orders the VIZIR to fetch the GUARDIAN of the Treasury. Together the six of them go to the scene of the theft.

SULTAN: Open the door to the Treasure Chamber! (The SULTAN enters and counts the sacks of gold. He misses four.) Where are the four missing sacks?

GUARDIAN: Your Majesty, I am as ignorant as you! I swear I haven't given my keys to anyone! I swear it by Heaven! (He falls on his knees in subjection.)

SULTAN (to the VIZIR and the three officials of the mosque): Do you have any idea how thieves might have gotten in here?

They examine the walls and corners, every nook, and can not find the slightest trace of their entry.

CLERK: He definitely did not touch the wall!

SULTAN: Reflect well! Tomorrow, if I ask you again, do not contradict me. Since you avow your ignorance, I will be able to tell you how the treasure was stolen!

VIZIR (to servants): Bring me some pottery fragments filled with burning embers!

He is going to get to the bottom of this. A servant brings him what he asked for, along with some straw. The VIZIR tells everyone to leave, lights the straw on the embers, closes the door carefully and leaves. They all go outside to watch the wall from the other side. The VIZIR watches intently, and he spies some smoke escaping from the part of the wall the thieves invaded. He cries out.

VIZIR: Here's where the swine got in!

With a blow of his fist he bashes in the repaired part of the wall, which has still not quite dried. The CROWD oohs and aahs.

CROWD: O Grand Vizir, may Allah smile upon your Father and Mother! You're the cleverest Berber who ever came down the pike!

The officials of the mosque are seized. The SULTAN returns to his mechouar, to consult with his LAW HEADS.

SULTAN: What does the law say about ripping off the Sultan's palace?

LAW HEADS (with perfectly legal bloodthirst): You must cut off their heads and exhibit them at the gates of the city! Crime against the State!

SULTAN (to VIZIR): Go with these scoundrels to get back the gold they stole. If any of them escape,

        I'll have <u>your</u> head as well!

The GAZELLES sadly march off, boxed in by the VIZIR and some soldiers. Once on the road, the VIZIR speaks to them casually.

VIZIR: Looks like the Sultan's going to initiate his reign with your heads, eh?

GAZELLES: O, Vizir, we are under the nose of God and no less under yours! Please advise us how to get out of this pickle!

VIZIR: Well, boys, that could possibly be arranged--for a fee!

GAZELLES: Name your fee, O Noble One! We've got plenty more than just the Sultan's lousy gold!

VIZIR: Well, then. It's simple. When the Sultan is about to . . . uh . . . decapitate you, just cross your fingers and say "King's X"!

GAZELLES: "King's X"? Are you out of your expanded mind?

VIZIR: No, no boys. Trust me. When the Sultan asks you what the hell do you mean, "King's X," you just tell him, "Our attorney, effendi, is your Vizir!"

Their mouths drop in comprehension. They load the VIZIR with gifts and jewels, and some charms. He also recovers the sacks of gold and takes them back to the SULTAN.
    Finally, the time comes to lop off their heads. The executioner stands high above them, flexing his axe--once, twice--and they cry out loud for justice! When the SULTAN hears this, he is furious. He orders them brought before him.

SULTAN: This is an outrage! To what justice

do you have the audacity to appeal?

GAZELLES: O Sultan, your Vizir will speak for us!

The SULTAN is astonished. Before he can gather his wits to assault the VIZIR, that worthy courtier has begun his defense.

VIZIR: Your Excellency, one does not decapitate men of such quality! No other Sultan could boast of any citizens nearly so subtle and artful! Show them mercy. One day they will be useful to you, and their services will be worth more than all the treasures in your coffers!

SULTAN: Bah! I don't have to listen to your learned drivel! If I let them go, they will go somewhere else and commit the same crimes!

VIZIR: If Your Excellency accords them a generous reprieve it will cause them to live honestly and keep them from ever more stealing!

SULTAN: I refuse to listen to another word of this rot! Besides, it is not I who order this punishment-- for I am the most generous of mortals--it is the law!

VIZIR: In that case, effendi, I'm afraid that the law says that <u>your</u> head must fall first!

SULTAN: What! How? This is nonsense!

VIZIR: You have also committed a crime against the State! Who went in to get the sacks? Who handed them out until they cried "Enough!"?

As they hear these words, the tribunal and assembled publicans applaud. They begin to move slowly toward the throne. The SULTAN'S eyes shift warily; he braces himself, then stands up, throws down his crown and stamps on it in a tantrum. He is swallowed up by the people.

Now that's working through the System!

Overheard in Casablanca

"O, Itto, won't you tell me your secret? How do you manage to keep your underarms so sweet with all these nasty foreigners around?"
"Simple, my dear. I use Magic! Works like a charm. . . ."
"Yes, friends, you too can repel the invader! Just send away to Universal By-Products--today! And, for you kids, we've got our special Junior Kit--snake charms with real buzz-flute and genuine defanged cobra . . . a hard-to-get Egyptian Tarot with E-Z instructions . . . and a full set of flaming pentagrams! Be the first kid in your tent to teleport! Get Mom and Dad to send away to Universal By-Products--today! That's Universal By-Products, right in the center of the Casbah, in Massat!"

If you consult your Arabian Nights you discover that all the magicians come from the Maghreb. They are Berbers. St. Augustine was a Berber, born in Algeria. Ibn el-Arabi and Yusuf of Andalusia ("The Wandering Dervish") were Berbers. The Berbers are heavy, get it? And they are the only people I've run across who turned their proud backs on "civilization" and stuck to the simple way. (Except hippies and Amish, of course.)

Their only concession to the Arab conquerors was the adoption of Islam. This doesn't mean much more than saying, OK, we believe you. The Berbers who stayed in the mountains heard little more from the long-nosed foreigners. The Arabs are simply not mountain people.

Berbers who copped out for the cities, of course, got fucked over. Arab style. That means you have to learn Arabic, which is a guaranteed headspin. It's not that it's hard. It's just the changes you have to put your head through to understand it. Indirect psychotherapy. The Arabs are crafty dudes. They never force more than adoption of Islam and the Arabic language when they conquer. There's your cultural offensive! (More on the Arabic language later.)

Naturally the Berbers were hip to this insidious imperialism of the mind. They fought like mad dogs. The Arabs used the desert like the British used the seas, and they are very skillful generals when they get it together. After only about a hundred years of resistance the Berbers by and large gave up. This meant they held their mountain strongholds and let the Arabs take the lowlands. So it took a strong-winded imperialist to lay anything on the mountain tribes. To this day there are enormous numbers of Berbers who don't know a single word of Arabic (not to mention French, Spanish, or English). Their languages are Tuareg, Tamazight, Chleuh, and like that. There are seven main ones in Morocco, mutually unintelligible. Since magic is language and language is magic, Berber magic has little relation to the Arab craft we learned about in Marrakech.

Learning about Arab <u>black</u> magic is easy as falling by your neighborhood herbalist. But as far as I can discover, there is no "black" art among the Berbers. For the everyday selfish Arab, magic depends on drawing energy from an "illegitimate" source—violating the Law of the Universe, but constructing an artificial world with its own limited energy source within. Berber magic always depends on trial by fire, initiation, and experience.

The Legend of Hamou bou Tekiout

He knew nothing but planting trees. Every year he planted, until finally, one year, overcome by travail, he picked up his pruning hook and cut off the live branch of a fig tree. He planted it, watered it, and swore this oath: "Tomorrow morning, when I come back, if you haven't bloomed, if you aren't absolutely <u>covered</u> with leaves and fruits, I'll beat the pips out of you with my pruning hook!"

And he went home to bed.

The next morning he went out to look at the branch, and he found a fig tree covered with leaves and ripe fruit. He climbed up and began to eat the fruits, then cried loudly, "Anyone who wants to eat some figs, come hither!"

An ogress heard him! She came beneath the tree and cried, "Throw me a fig!"

He threw her one.

"Throw me another. One will never satisfy me!"

He threw her another.

"Come on, give me a handful!"

He plucked a bunch, attached them to the end of his pruning hook, and lowered them down to her.

"How cold!" she said cunningly. "I can't take them with my delicate hands. Give them to me with yours!"

He picked off another bunch and handed them down to her, but she ignored the fruit, seized him by the arm, pulled him out of the tree, and stuffed him into her sack! She carried him on her back all the way to her lair.

Hamou bou Tekiout thought fast. He cried out: "The voice of an angel inspires me! It says whoever does not do his prayers at this spot runs the risk of being abducted!" At these words the ogress put down her sack and said her devotions. During her prayers, Hamou bou Tekiout crept out of the sack, filled it up with sand, put a lizard on top, and returned to his fig tree.

When the ogress had finished her prayers she took up the sack again, believing Hamou was still inside, and brought it home to her children. She opened it, plunged in her hand to take out her prisoner, and got a nasty lizard bite!

"It's that son of a dog Hamou bou Tekiout that did this!" she swore.

She retraced her steps and found Hamou up in his fig tree once more, crying, "Who wants some figs?"

She shouted up, "Give me one!" He handed her a fig, but she caught his arm, yanked him down, and carried him off to her children once again.

"We'll keep him for a few days," she cackled to her children, "and have some fun!"

They kept stuffing him with food, and he grew fat and meaty. One day the ogress pinched the flesh on his shoulders, found it good and plump, and crowed to her children: "He's fat enough! We can get ready to cook him, and we'll have a feast!" The little ones went off searching for wood and came back to light up the oven. The ogress put an ember at the mouth of the oven and told Hamou, "Blow on it to start the fire!"

"I'm sorry, but my grandmother only taught me how to play the flute and repair my shoes!" he replied sulkily.

So the ogress bent down to light the oven herself, and as she was bending--Hamou pushed her into the fire! It consumed her in a puff. He then caught the children, who tried to run away, and grilled them one after another. Afterward, he went into their lair and ripped it off.

He left not knowing where to go. When he tired of just wandering around he spotted a fog lifting, and betook himself that way. He walked and walked, crossed a desert, and finally arrived at a walled town whose gates were closed for the night.

Hamou was very tired, so he stretched out to sleep on the gate sill, saying, "I will enter at dawn, when they open the gates."

Now it just so happened that the king of this town was about to die, and the citizens were disputing among themselves, all wishing to succeed him. (Berber kings do not transmit the right to rule hereditarily.) The townsmen wisely decided that since everyone wanted to be king they would choose the first stranger they found outside the gates in the morning.

Dawn. The people and notables of Makhzen come to the gate. They order the gatekeeper to open it. He swings open the gate and the townspeople nearly trip over the body prone on the sill. They wake him up. "Wake up! Get up!" they cry. "Allah has blessed you!"

Hamou was frightened, thinking they wanted to take him to the king and chop off his head. "By Allah! What have I done? What do you want with me?"

"Do not be frightened! Allah smiles on you today!" They took him to the mechouar, showed him the throne, and said: "You are our new king! You have no relatives here, thus no axes to grind. You will punish the wrongdoers, release the innocent, and govern according to the dictates of Divine Justice!"

They held a great festival in his honor. When they wanted to publish the news of his investiture in the marketplace, they asked him his name.

"Nobody should blush at his name," he answered. "Only a fool can disavow his own. My name is Hamou, the Man with the Braid!"

"Long live Hamou, the Man with the Braid!" the people cried.

They presented the vizir to the new king, gave him the keys to the city, showed him the granaries, the stables, and the royal treasuries. They feasted for weeks upon weeks, gradually returning to their normal affairs.

Hamou governed according to his good sense and sharp wit, and the people say he was a good and wise king.
                                           --Beni Touzine

Since the Arab conquest, of course, there has been a mélange of magic and legend. The Berbers handle it in their own inimitable way.

The Birth of the Prophet

According to the Berbers, this is what came to pass when Allah caused the Prophet Mohammed to be born.

A man got married and eventually had a son who went eight days without nursing. The mother held a festival, where she gathered all the women of the town, hoping to find a wetnurse who could make him feed. When they had all convened, each one tried without success.

Meanwhile, a Berber man, his wife, and son were riding slowly down the road on a camel.

"Look! Some people having a fiesta!" exclaimed the woman. "Let's go over and ask for alms!" They ordered the camel to bend down so she could dismount. She went off to beg, leaving her husband with the child.

"May Allah bless you!" she proclaimed to the crowd of mothers. "Please give me charity for the love of God!" This canny woman knew Arabs give alms freely.

"Woman," said the mistress of the house, "I implore you in the name of Allah and of your God, try to nurse my son!"

The Berber woman came forward, took the infant, gave him her breast, and the child suckled it!

"O beggar woman!" exclaimed the mothers excitedly. "You remain here with us and we'll take care of all your needs!"

She hurried back to tell her husband. "They asked me to stay here to nurse a baby!"

"God's grace!" he exclaimed. "We could never find a better deal! Let's go!" They remounted their camel and rode into the village, where the people gave them a house and care of the child.

Some time elapsed and the little child grew. One

day, the beggar woman's son said to her, "Please let my new brother go out with me to look after the sheep!"

"But, my son, what if he should get sunstroke?"

"I'll build him a little shelter!"

At morning the woman gave them their lunch and they set off. The two brothers played happily, high in the green, sunny hills. But while the young shepherd was busy gathering his herd, all of a sudden Allah and the Archangel Gabriel descended from Heaven, seized and killed the young infant, extracted his heart and liver, washed them, and put them back into place! The shepherd saw them flashing off and ran like lightning to tell his mother.

"Mother," he cried, "some country thugs have killed my brother!"

"Aaughh! Sit down and shut up, child! We must wait for your father, and flee!"

The father soon returned and was informed. "We must save ourselves!" he declared. "Before anyone finds out! Quickly, quickly!" They fled immediately.

On their way, the woman suddenly got a flash. "Let's see the place where they slaughtered our poor one!"

They returned to the pasture and found the child playing happily by his shelter!

"My Little One!" exclaimed the woman. "He's not dead at all!" She turned to her husband. "Let's give him back to the townspeople right away!" He agreed and they returned to the village to ask the real mother to take him back.

So the child was returned to his natural mother. But just two years later, both his parents died. Orphaned.

Luckily, a wealthy gentleman took pity on him and asked the young boy to tend his sheep. He entered the gentleman's service, and the flock could not but grow and prosper, for Allah had favored the young shepherd with virtue and sanctity. One day, though, after the boy inadvertently lost a goat, his master beat him black and blue and left him for dead. A compassionate Berber widow saw him and took pity. She offered to take him in.

"You'll only have to take my mule to Marrakech."

"If I am strong enough," he answered gratefully. He was.

A while later some of the inhabitants of Marrakech decided to undertake a strenuous journey. In those days, far out in the desert, lived an old hermit who was reputed to be a prophet. The travelers organized their camel caravan, planning to pass through the prophet's region. The young child showed up to ride with them, a splendid light radiating from his presence. The others attributed it to a little too much to smoke.

Along the way one of the men smacked the child in the face and made him cry. Allah at once plunged the entire caravan into a thick dark. The astonished men stopped and loudly proclaimed their faith in God.

"Who among us has committed such a sin worthy of this chastisement?" they cried.

"I did," cried one of them in terror. "I hit this child!"

They took up a young kid-goat and sacrificed it at the feet of the young boy. The darkness began to clear up.

As the sun reappeared a small cloud formed over the head of the young child, protecting him from the arduous heat. They journeyed thus to the house of the hermit-prophet and asked his hospitality.

"Welcome!" he cried heartily, for hospitality is the law of the desert.

He invited them in, one by one. The little child was left for last, the cloud still protecting him.

"Come in!" said the hermit, and as the child entered, the cloud dissolved. The hermit knew immediately that the child was blessed by Allah. He gave him a private room and served him the evening meal personally. At sunup, they prepared to go off. The child remounted his camel, and no sooner was he up than the cloud reformed over his head, throwing a protective shadow.

"When you return," said the hermit, "may it please you to rest with me again!"

So on the way back they stopped there again. The old man welcomed them and ushered them in. When the child entered, again last, the little cloud, which had followed him all the way, dissipated. The hermit slaughtered some cattle in their honor and served them a sumptuous feast.

Once their hunger was slaked they wished to take their leave. The hermit quickly gripped the child's garments.

"Why do you grasp at me?" asked the child. "Can you not see that my companions await outside?"

"Do you not know the reason? I beg you to assure me the possession of the seven houses of Paradise!"

"By Allah! Who am I to do such a thing?"

"You are the Prophet chosen by God! I will not release you until you satisfy my request!"

"Done! I agree, but I advise you to keep it a secret. Otherwise, Allah will blind you!"

As the caravan was about to leave the hermit took after them. He kept repeating: "There is no God but Allah, and Mohammed is his Prophet!" He pointed to the child. "And he is the Prophet!" They stopped in astonishment, and prayed.

The child, radiating, filled a vase with some water from a clear stream. He washed his hands in it and a rose appeared.

--Imerghan

The Berber-Bedouins of the south of Morocco have a saying. When you undertake to do anything for anyone outside your tribe you first warn him by saying: "Debt blackened the raven!" By the Berbers, the porcupine was once a Jewish ironmonger who made arrows. At the market he overvaunted the value of his merchandise and was changed into an arrow-beast. The Arabs say, "The friendship of a Berber is like plowing a swamp!" There is always something valuable for the Muslim to reap. Put all this together and you end up with a people who eat macrobiotically and say their prayers.

Scene: Dawn in a small Berber village, high in the
Rif. We zero in on a mud house. The WOMEN and OLD MEN
open the heavy doors to the first ray of sun, and greet
their spirits.

WOMEN and
OLD MEN: We Salute you, O Guardian of our Circle!
           A good morning to you and your ancestors;
           A good morning to your saints and protectors;
           A good morning to the Sublime Porte of the East!

OLD MEN: Help us! Protect our children against the evil eye,
           And keep them from harm!
           Let those absent return in good health!

WOMEN: Do not ever forsake us, we implore!
           We shall never stop serving you
           With all faith and without second thoughts!

    A key to the Berber's freedom turns in the magical lock on his door. Each house lies under the watchful aura of a familiar spirit—perhaps embodied in the family cat or pet serpent. He is called the <u>assassin buhham</u>: the Guardian of the Household. Each family has <u>its own special</u> spirits (the armies of Heaven are limitless). It is a heinous crime to mistreat the cat or the serpent, or to mutilate the tribe's sacred almond tree.
    At the festival of Ain el-Mouloud, the Berber women burn branches of <u>tiftilin</u> in honor of the family spirits. They soak the branches in <u>a special</u> herbal oil, then ignite them at the base of the walls and high in the branches of the sacred tree.
    A Berber's home is literally his castle. Psychically and physically. To move in he doesn't just sign a lease and have the gas and phone hooked up. The women fill three pitchers: one with water, one with oil, and one with wheat. They get a ewe at the market. They put on their finest clothes. At bedtime they push the

ewe toward the house, following tolbas--magicians--who recite
prayers and create the atmosphere for harmonious involvement with
the familiar spirits. At the threshhold, they slay the ewe and
sprinkle the doorway with her blood, followed by the water, wheat,
and oil. Only then do they enter, spraying the place with incense
and herbal perfume. The tolbas come in last, to sit on mats the
women have spread. They sit up all night singing and reciting the
Koran. In the morning they serve a meal to the tolbas, who transmit
the baraka--the blessing.

The house in a Berber tribe actually resembles a medieval
castle. It is always isolated, by clever landscaping, so that it
never looks onto another dwelling, even though they may be only
twenty feet apart. It is entirely possible to pass a whole Berber
village and never know it at all, so adept are they at artifice.
The house itself is square, with one door, and high, narrow windows
in the walls. These walls are usually twenty feet thick, rammed
earth--a communal fortress with a heavy occult barrier around it.
Each tighremt (communal castle) has four towers, facing the cardinal
points, which store grain and provide lookout.

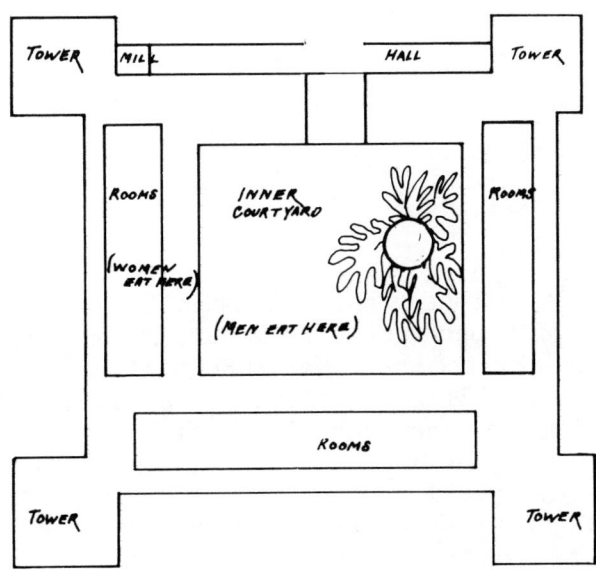

Berber homes are always communal. Two or three families generally live in one tighremt. If a stranger wants to move into a tighremt he brings an offering of eggs and chickens, has tea, meets the folks, and ceremonially asks if his family can move in too. If it's all right with the actual inhabitants, the newcomer gets his family together and moves right in. He helps out until he doesn't want to anymore, then he must move out.

The Peace Corps came around once, disguised as well-meaning ex-basketball players, and nearly flipped out when they smelled the shitpile growing just outside the Berbers' houses. "Filth!" they cabled back to Washington, who smiled benignly and replied, "Teach them." The volunteers spit on their hands and rolled up their pants, and looked up to find a ring of seventy-eight Berbers each pointing a matchlock rifle straight at their flabby guts.

"But it's filthy here!" they squealed in explanation.

"Go!"

"But we came all the way from Washington! With special counterinsurgency training at Chiapas! I mean, after all!"

"Go!"

"But, look, what about these shitpiles?"

"Fertilizer!"

The volunteers clutched their stomachs and fainted dead away.

The Jackal and the Goat

A goat left the trail and climbed an oak near the bank of a pond. A jackal came along and saw the goat's reflection in the water. He plunged into the pond.

"Ooof! This is water, you stinking goat!"

When he recovered his foolish head he saw the goat in the tree. He went over to the tree and explained sheepishly, "I thought you were drowning!"

Overcome by emotion, the goat came out of the tree and the jackal ate him.

--Ait Sgougou

OR: When he recovered and saw the goat in the tree, he went over and said that jackals, goats, and lambs had been officially reconciled.

The goat replied: "From up here in the tree I can see some horses and greyhounds coming this way. No doubt they will want to come to the reunion as well!"

The jackal fled without further ado.

--Ouargha

OR: When he recovered and saw the goat he pleaded, "Come on down and we can say our prayers together!"

"OK," said the goat, "but first go and get the imam!"

"Where is he?"

"At the foot of the tree!"

The jackal looked and found a greyhound--and he hauled ass out of there!

"Hey, I thought you wanted to come and pray!" cried the goat after him.

"I'll come back, but I'm right in the middle of my bath!"

--Akhsass

The Jackal and the Lion

The jackal and the lion made a pact to go out and plunder. By nighttime, though, they hadn't found anything, and they went to sleep on the edge of a cliff.

The jackal said to the lion, "Uncle, I'm far enough away from the edge, aren't I?"

"No, you fool, you're right on top of it!"

When the lion fell asleep, the jackal crept around behind him.

"Help, help! I'm falling!" he cried.

Not realizing the jackal had changed position, the lion jumped up and fell off the edge. The jackal ran off, but the lion managed to save himself. He ran after his cur cousin and caught him by the tail, which he bit in two.

"Curse you, cousin!" growled the lion. "We'll be able to recognize you from now on!"

—Zemmour

A Berber Pun

A man prepared to go to market. His daughter asked him, "Father, bring me back a scarf (tassast)."

He put on his burnous and left. Near the marketplace he stopped to rest. Suddenly the Caliph appeared, mounted on his camel. Our man rose to do reverence. The Caliph's camel got frightened, bucked, and threw the potentate. The guards seized the man, flogged him, and threw him into prison. That afternoon they let him go.

Back at home, his daughter asked, "By Allah, Father, have you remembered to bring the scarf I asked for?"

"I've got seventy scarves for you, my daughter!" he answered.

(Tassast means both a head scarf and a whip wound.)

These Berbers: no flies on them. For one thing, who knows where they've been? We saw one Berber girl who looked just like an Irish Catholic: pug nose, freckles, red hair, and green eyes. There are tribes full of blond, blue-eyed, slender quiz kids. In the Rif Mountains you meet Berbers with long, straight black hair, high cheekbones, and long, thin faces, resembling a taucross between a Greek and a Sikh. You find black Berbers in the north of Morocco and pasty whites (and even a tribe of blues! honest!) in the south.

So what makes them <u>Berbers</u>? They're the <u>natives</u> around these parts, that's all. Their own legends put them as the original inhabitants since the ruins of time. There are suggestions of a prehistory in Atlantis, borne out by certain occult investigations. Put your faith in them if you are so inclined. Scholastically, they are still a complete mystery, since everyone dismisses them as primitive headshrinkers.

How do they relate to us gringos? That's the question. They could sure learn a lot from us. Why, if they had any good old-fashioned <u>ambition</u>, some <u>gumption</u>, they could get <u>jobs</u> sweeping up after the <u>Arab</u> men who <u>sit</u> around in the cafes <u>all</u> day studying human weakness. You got to start somewhere! But no, they'd rather live in <u>communes</u>, for Christ's sake, and let their hair grow long and <u>filthy</u>, and keep off to themselves! Oh, they're nice enough if you get to <u>know</u> them, I s'pose, long as they don't <u>smell</u>!

An' I <u>heerd</u> they got some pretty <u>wayout</u> dances and <u>what-all</u>! But I tell ya something. Don't let them hear ya saying <u>anything</u>. They'll kick yer ass as lief as look at ya. And they're <u>tough</u>! Why, I heerd 'bout a bunch of Berber fellers had it out with a gang of cowboys from Boise--they done went and <u>kicked ass</u>! An' they's talk that they mighta put some kinda <u>hex</u> on the pokes, too! Nossir! Wouldn't mess with no Berbers!

Our Ingenuous Ancestors

A long time ago some men got into a quarrel. One killed another. They let the murderer go without taking vengeance, until one day, when he went away on a short trip, they set up an ambush for him on the return road.

The man got a vibe and said to himself, "They are surely waiting for me in ambush." So he took another road, which passed right in front of his enemies' tents.

They waited and waited in vain, until dark, and they finally went back home. When the men arrived at their tents the women announced, "He came back this way!"

"May he go in peace from now on!" they responded. "For he is under our protection now that he has passed before our tents!"

--Ait Sadden

There's a trick to it: everyone doesn't have to be alike! Even if we successfully strongarm a revolution we automatically embrace a hostile contingent. We can't just kill them off--it ain't dainty. We have to draw our own magic circle.

Berber enclaves generate much more energy by sympathetic induction than Nixon does by his bogus press conferences, SST's, Chiefs of Staff, and Chinas. "The will of the People is stronger than Man's tricknology!"

"So, well, how do you do it?" we ask. That's the whole trip, longhairs! A little American know-how comes in handy now. A recycling, self-contained, but open-ended contraption to harness the rushing tide of thought power. Send it down to Psychic Engineering (and don't forget some kind of self-governor). Later someone discovers Berbers and orchids have done it that way for thousands of years. "My, my. Ain't Nature smart!"

High energy trips. The power of thought, the power of change, the power of chance, the power of meaning. Here's a couple of Berber parabolic reflections on these very subjects:

Aguelmam Azigza (The Pond of Blue-green Waters)

  Once upon a time the land was inhabited by the Ait Ammar. They dug a well and covered it with a heavy hatch, fearing they might be flooded by the abundant waters.
  In those days the plain was surrounded by a forest full of lions. A woman, Itto oult Ammar, drawing water from the well one day at sunset heard the roar of a lion. She was frightened, took flight, and in her haste she forgot to put the cover back onto the well. The water overflowed, flooded the encampment, and sloped off in the direction of the tribe of the Blue Men (Azigza). Today the spring called Ansar Aoussar flows from this spot.

  --Ait Sgougou

A Dream

  A man had a dream. The next morning he met someone he did not like. He called out: "May Allah bless you, stop a moment. Listen to the dream I had last night, and give me the key to understanding it."
  "What was your dream?"
  "I was sleeping--Allah never slumbers!--when I saw myself with one foot on one mountain and the other foot on another, and between the two there was a pass."
  The man reflected a moment. He said, "A lion will attack you and tear you in two, one piece here and the other there!" He went off leaving the dreamer worried and anxious.
  Where was a friend? He spotted one on the road and hailed him.
  "What's the matter?" the friend asked. "Are you ill? You look completely different!"
  "My friend, I am not sick. My depression stems from

a dream I had and the interpretation someone gave me."

"What was your dream?"

The man related the dream.

The friend said sadly: "If you had not revealed your dream to that badmouth, I would have told you that you would become a chief, that you would govern two tribes, one foot on the one and one foot on the other. But now, my friend, you must learn that a dream only confides in one person! Much as it grieves me, that which was said will come true! Adieu!"

Indeed, that was exactly what happened.

—Ait Ayyach

Maybe the first step is to gather the trustworthy and count blessings collectively. And no double-counting! Then some kind of group tattooing. Cast a mental gland in the direction of the worthy one, mankind. Help this sore afflicted king. Align him with the Infinite, feed him with experience, care for him with subtle energy. Don't advertise our dreams; interpret them. Catch the Ineffable in an ineffable cup. Pour, quivering, from one gold goblet to another, treading land, treading water, temperate.

The Berbers raise a warning palm against building a fortress of words.

A Man and His Basket

A man of the Ait Bou Harazen went up a high ridge to warm himself in the sun. When he was no longer cold he decided to make a basket and gather some almonds. The harvest that year had been especially rich. He took a long needle, threaded it, and began to sew up strands of dwarf palm. First he made the base, then the linings. When he had sewn up to the height of his left shoulder, he turned around and did the other side, not realizing that he was enclosing himself in his own basket. When he had finished he couldn't figure out how to get himself free.

His children came, saw his predicament, and cried. Well-meaning people gathered around the basket. Each one had a piece of advice. One woman came and said, "You all have long hair and beards, but now it looks like they don't do you any good!"

"So what do you think we should do?" they inquired.

"Simple. Roll the basket down a hill and it will break, releasing the man trapped inside!"

"Your advice is most sage," they agreed, and they pushed the basket down the slope.

When it reached the bottom they rushed down to look. The man was a bloody pulp and the basket fairly intact.

--Ntifa

Another guideline:

A Simpleton

A man whose wife had died raised a small boy. When the child had grown up the father asked him what skill he'd like to learn. After reflection, the young man decided to apprentice himself to a blacksmith.

When he had learned some elements of the trade he said to his father, "Prepare my shop!" The father furnished him with tools, but the boy was so clumsy that his hands and feet soon got covered with burns.

One day, tired of this life, he asked his father's new wife to prepare him a bath. He washed his whole body and the next morning dressed himself in his finest clothes. He set off to market to buy some shoes. He had never owned a pair in his life. Along the way he met some other young men who taunted him as a yokel, made faces, and generally threw him into confusion. When he got to the market he bought some old shoes, put them under his arm, and started back home.

On the road he found a goat's foot. He picked it up and examined it curiously, without paying attention to where he was walking. His foot stubbed on a big rock with such force that his toe exploded! He said to himself, "Thank God the blow struck my toe and not my new shoes!"

—Ntifa

The Story of a Tortoise

The Ait Bou Oulli hunted. They once found a tortoise, picked him up, and passed him around. They didn't know what he was because when you pick up a tortoise he draws his head and feet into his shell.

"Let's take it to the amghar," they decided. "He'll surely know what it is."

They took it to the local chief of soldiers. He turned it over and over, and finally declared: "I'm not a wise man, but I don't lack intelligence. This is the amulet of Moulay Mohammed! We'll draw lots and each of us in turn will keep this valuable talisman at his house for one night. This way the baraka will spread over our works and the works of our children!" So they drew lots.

The man who drew the shortest lot took the tortoise home. He chose a beautiful pot, cleaned it, wrapped the "amulet" in fine silk, and poked it into the pot. Night and silence fell. The tortoise gingerly slid from the pot and crawled away. In the morning they couldn't find the "amulet." The man went to the mosque and told the story to his fellow tribesmen.

"By Allah! You've got bad karma, or something. We gave you that thing to bring good luck. If you don't find it, we're going to ransack your house!" Hearing these words, the man left the village.

Approaching a broad plain, he saw a group of shepherds who were playing with something that looked suspiciously like the "amulet." He went up to them and asked, "What's that?"

"A tortoise!" they answered.

He joined their game, and when they went back to rejoin their flocks he took the tortoise and returned to his village. He showed it to his tribesmen.

"Great! That's the amulet! Where'd you find it?"

"No, you're wrong!" he announced, amused at their ignorance. "This is merely a tortoise! Come and see for yourselves!"

But the men thought he was just trying to keep the "amulet" for himself. They grabbed it from him and told him to shove his nonsense. When he persisted and tried to snatch the tortoise back, they banished him forever.

--Ntifa

Assorted facts about Berbers: they only eat meat on market day, usually doing quite nicely on couscous, beans, carrots, pumpkin, pimento, raisins, figs, and a mutton soup called harira. Quite a yang diet for Morocco. The men would be insulted to carry wood for a woman, but quite happy to do her laundry. The French prescribed milk of magnesia for the Berbers, who thought it was poison. That Berber nation I mentioned was back in the eleventh century.

"Facts, facts, facts!" said Mr. Hassan Gradgrind. "Facts, facts, facts!" repeated Mr. Ali Bounderby. Bah. It grows late. We have been in Morocco six months. It is wonderful, incredible, all the adjectives. Unknown. Sublime. We are supercharged with the ancient past, the future meets us at the present. Things remain to be done. A period of receptivity, then a period of action. We must equalize. The oxygen masks drop from the subconscious overhead cupboard. A stewardess is on the inner loudspeaker.

This glorious trip in Morocco has to end--physically, at any rate. We are at the far stretch of our psychic plasma--out of our domain (learning, to be sure). But new impressions and subconscious information must be processed. The memory banks can overload temporarily, leading to half-a-dozen headspins. We must meet East with West. So we think.

We go to a friendly bazaar. The merchant knows us well; we have been staking out the joint for a few days previous, buying time, preparing for the bargaining joust. I've told him my best Arabic stories, admired his land and the heart of his people, assured him that his climate is just as good as California, if not better. We are ready for action.

"Ahh, my friend, welcome. Please come in!" He is all smiles, for he has picked up the vibes.

"Good morning, Ahmed. It goes well for you?"

"Yes, yes, no complaints! For you and your wife? Allah comforts you?"

"Yes, praise Allah!" We shake hands, touching our hearts.

"Billah, you are looking for something today, no?"

"You are clever, Ahmed. Perhaps we will be interested in something today, yes!"

"A caftan for your wife? A _pouf_, perhaps? Sheepskins? I have some beautiful new rugs, handwoven, from Rabat. . . ."

"We'll look around."

"Ah, please, my friend! I would be honored if you would have tea with me, in the back room! Can it not be so?"

"Thank you, Ahmed, you are very kind." We are escorted to the back room, thick with carpets. Ahmed produces a small gold table, handtooled with Arabic letters woven into incredible Islamic patterns. He goes out and returns a moment later with a beaten copper tinned teapot, steaming with mint tea, and three glasses. He pours carefully and with love.

"Now, my friend," he says, when we have all sipped and sighed.

"Ahmed, we are looking for something--very unusual!"

"Ah. I comprehend. I have some--a very little--of the _majoom_ left. . . ."

"No, no--not dope. We are needed elsewhere. We have already converted our dirhams on the black market, and we now look to-- _grease the skids_, we say in English."

"I do not comprehend."

"Ahmed, I have some words here, written by a very important

man in your country. We are looking for a <u>flying carpet</u>!" I hand him a folded paper. He reads it and rolls a cigarette.

"I may smoke?" he asks.

"Of course."

He inhales slowly, eyes fixed on the Arabic curls, and exhaling he shifts his eyes to us.

"This is very unusual."

"Yes."

"Come back tomorrow, very early. Perhaps I will have something for you."

The next morning, just after daybreak, we are back at Ahmed's shop. He hands us a bulky package.

"May Allah calm you, my friends!" he cries emotionally.

"Peace unto you!"

With a blessing, we depart.

V

LESSONS: FOR THE BODY, FOR THE MIND, FOR THE SOUL, FOR THE SPIRIT

Our magic carpet put in for refueling at Madrid (we dashed into
the Prado for an hour with Bosch), Paris (we lurked about the Gare
du Nord looking for an onion soup) and finally Amsterdam, where
we had thought to, uh, well, you know, uh, see what was happening. . . .
    We listened to old rock-and-roll on the Dam (the Gremlins had
taken over), got bitten by a "watcher" (if a dog is twice
the size of a normal dog, it's still a dog; if it's a million times
normal size, it's something new), learned that if we rented this
particular flat we couldn't go out into the garden (neighbors might
complain), looked into buying a houseboat gently floating on
luscious Dutch turds, ate lumpia and drank beer instead, learned
to read Dutch in three days (appartementen te huur), walked and
paid and paid and Oh, my God, if it isn't my old college chum
Corky Troy! What are you up to? Driving to England tomorrow.
Want to come?
    So Fate takes up again, smooth as another magic carpet (ours
had only gone as far as Paris and we'd taken an ordinary train to
Amsterdam, though enough of the magic rubbed off to conjure a

compartment in a full wagon) and before we know what, we are at
the Hook of Holland, laughing and eating that fine cheese. A
bright orange VW, splendiferous. Sailing the North Sea picking
up old threads and spinning new.

It was inevitable, I thought, as we sped down those glorious
English country lanes toward London. I recalled dozens and dozens
of clues we'd picked up in Morocco--how this friend was in London,
how they had cheap charter flights from London, how the British
Museum was the only place in Europe with information on certain
Atlantean obscurities. What the hell had we been thinking about
Amsterdam for anyway? Fucking inevitable.

Now here we are, fresh out of this bizarre red land where
they still ride on <u>donkeys</u>, for Christ's sake, where it takes you
two days to buy a <u>shirt</u>, and we're getting into freeways and
flyovers and we don't even really know the money. Time to begin
reorienting. Or is that reoccidenting?

Oh, yeah, I confess. In Morocco we had begun to crave some
"Western culture," whatever that is. I mean, the only film we
had seen in months was about the Arabian Beatles, a group called
"Meganeen" ("Meg meg meg meg . . . meg meg . . . Meganeen!").
Loosely translated, that means "Idiots." More than that, though.
We had undergone dehypnotism but hadn't yet seen the underground
chamber where they cut your legs off, stuff the cracks with Sahara
sand, and put them back together but not <u>quite</u> truly. The Berbers--
ah, the Berbers!--had sparked some ancient music within, but their
lesson was in tight-knittedness. Our deep reason for leaving
Morocco was--"After all, this is not our domain." We could have
had a magnificent villa in Tangier for twenty dollars a month.
But it just simply is not our scene, that decadent expatriate
Tangier scene where they talk about Paris in the twenties and
swap wives and cluck their grandmotherish tongues when one of
their cronies in Rome gets busted ("Oh, yeah, they kicked him out
of Spain a few years ago, too . . ."). We wanted <u>action, results,
happenings</u>. We had received. Now we were going to, well, I don't
know. How did we know our mental equipment was suitable to meet
the needs we so clearly understood? Recurring thought: if only
all our friends were here, it would be different. If this, if
that. Let's get it together to get it together to get it together
to . . .

BULLSHIT! You just have to DO it!

So we split. Our direction was vaguely back home. The <u>I Ching</u>

advised us to cross the great water but stop halfway for a time. Circumstance had soapcaked us wet into England. A good place to make connections, eh wot?

"Hey, watch out man, they drive on the left here!" Corky shouted as I crept into the future of some oncoming traffic. Driving was going to take concentration, I could see. I swerved back at an eternal pace and missed a car by the will of Allah. Insane to drive when you can walk. Just gets you there faster and who needs that? Monorail, public transport, astral projection, Berber tolbas who fix on their goal and run top speed for 24 hours and aren't even winded. . . .

"Hey, man, get over to the fucking left!!" Narrowly avoid another one, still undismayed. Let's see now, London. . . . They got these damned roundabouts all the time, drive left, drive left, tenez la gauche, links fahren, drive left, drive left. . . .

Haven't driven a thing in six months. Rented bicycles once in Marrakech. Learned Moroccan traffic pattern: "Insh'allah!" As Allah wills. It works. Does the whole nation have to agree to the spell, though? That's one of the things we'll discover in England. Can you transplant Morocco? You can't export dirhams.

Corky asks how's my career going. I flash on Barrie Stevens, who said, "I don't want a career, I want a careen." Don't confuse yourself with your credentials. Nevertheless, it energizes thoughtforms dropped into subconsciousness: steady progression, climbing a straight mountain; falling into an underground ravine. Hip, radical, straight--all those words. Did the essential self change? It is still a center of experience, a crosswire of the universe. Inductance rising, to be sure. Arabian wire-strippers did their job and now how to fit it into the schematic.

Alchemical marriage: Morocco was so jaded Red and now England is so bloody Green. An instructor, or ox-goad, sits on cubical stone in front of tightly drawn purple veil hung from two gray stone pillars. He wears red robe with green yoke. The cuffs of his blue undergarment just peek out. His right hand holds a broadsword high, his left a balance scale low. A burst of primal energy shoots through him, filtered first through Aries and afterward through Pisces. He is Justice, he is Lamed. He will see to it that we do right. We have no say in the matter, other than to say "Yes."

Morocco would work itself into a new scene. No point in forcing.

We whirlicrawl through Wapping Old Stairs, John O'Groats, Simpson's-in-the-Straw, Millrace-upon-Titheringae, Sheep's Dip, Purslane, Thresher, Cliffhang Common, Old Potbelly Road, and Chancre Town. Joyous Olde Englande commences our integration, and anyway I do believe it's the main waystation on the Hashish Trail. The Superior Man does not change his direction. (The English <u>I Ching</u> calls him "The Civ'lised Man.")

We're coming into north London now, yek. Well, blow me down! There's Fish and Chips, 2/6, just like at H. Salt's in Berkeley. We'll just stop a bit, eh wot. A spot of English food.

MEMORY: A week of freaking on brown Berber barley bread. I sit at my desk in Tangier, watching the sun drop behind the ancient city, a black green sky, the evening star rising. My back is to the bookcase against the wall, loaded with history of the Sassanids, Islamic art, Golden Boughs, Tales of the Dervishes-- potent. Our friend S'bits performs his sunset prostrations to Allah outside on the broad green meadow. Suddenly, <u>talons</u> clutch the back of my neck! I reach up, slapping, but find nothing there! The clawing persists and I feel a weight dropping onto my upper back, <u>entering through my neck joint and taking over my spine</u>!!

"Holy Jesus," I think wildly, "it's that fucking hash!"

I start to go crosseyed and feel a deep well of malice drilling upward into consciousness.

From that moment I am a Tasmanian devil, finding fault, lashing and crabbing, snarling and snapping, crosseyed in the mind. The tiny scrap of sanity I have retained huddles for safety in the back of my brain. I cannot write, talk, walk, or think without snarling. Anyone I speak to has their evolution retarded at least thirty years. Tangier sighs in relief when I finally fall into bed that night, exhausted as a madman.

The next morning I wake up shitting and continue

shitting until noon. I am completely and wholly wiped out, a wet djellaba. The malice has changed to self-pity. I insist on calling a specialist.

The doctor takes one look at me and smiles. "You've got dysentery," he says matter-of-factly. "Fast for twenty-four hours and take these, four a day."

We go into Fish and Chips and a bloated countermaid greets us. "'Ello, luvs, what'll yer 'ave?"

"I'll have the roe and chips, please," I say, well aware that one lesson didn't take yet. Corky and Barbara order more sensibly, but not much.

The awareness of the latent lesson is surely the first step. It remains to remold the physical shell. Dysentery had taught me there is more to food than taste. Even though Berber barley bread was wholesome and delicious, it did not relate to my whole system. Eating is not habit. Eating is not punching a stomach clock. In fact, it is drawing regenerative substance from the Earth, which has been fertilized by the Sun, in order to rebear the conscious cells of our bodies. H'rumph. What you eat determines how you will regenerate. It does not change the essential self, but streamlines the self's possessions. (The menu at The Seed restaurant in London calls itself "Tomorrow's You.")

I felt better reading a poster they had up at Fish and Chips, something to the effect that "Fish is the only animal that is not raised for food. It is caught wild from the deep, cold sea." Now I see where they're trying aquaculture (the ubiquitous and all-venal They).

We stuffed our foolish bellies and carried on. Friends--actual friends--to stay with in Wimbledon.

Mirja was a Finnish Aries and Gypsy a Swiss Virgo. We had met them in Marrakech and had fallen in like true sons and daughters of the Trail. We had told them where to score. They had turned us on and provided tape cassette music--a rare and envied commodity in foreign parts. They were stinking rich and quite generous. We had had brief but intense rendezvous with them in Marrakech, trading first impressions like we used to flip baseball cards. We all exchanged addresses and kisses on Moroccan hassocks after a sumptuous splurge, and Barbara and I dashed off to catch the bus for the Rif. Up to this point it was all pleasant memory and pleasanter expectation. We were actually toying with the idea of making it up to Finland one of these days. As we stayed on in northern Morocco, they left for England. We sent postcards and even telephoned a couple of times.

From Amsterdam we phoned for real. We were coming in the next day. They squealed with excitement and the words bounced like rubber baby-buggy bumpers. "Wimbledon Park . . ." "in time for dinner . . ." "can't fucking wait, mon . . ."

We were cutting around east London to avoid the plague. I flashed on dog carts and four wheelers, hansom cabs and Inverness capes, "a sticky wicket in the Bayswater Road!" Through Junctions, Greens, and Commons, follow the tennis signs, remember how we would walk down to the port in Tangier, slowly past the small plaza rich with orange blossoms and jasmine? From the top of the hill you could see a snatch of Mediterranean blue and sometimes a white boat would be perfectly framed between the trees and minarets. . . .

"Keep left, goddamn it!" Oh, yeah. That traffic shit again. Right. We're in England. London. Jesus. Be nice to see Mirja and Gypsy. Talk about Morocco.

We find it. It is a magnificent old Gothic house in a block of old Gothic houses, in a village of old Gothic houses, shady greens and deer-filled parks. They rent the upper floors from a Pakistani family below.

Ah! Great slobbers and squeezes disturb the evening's chapati. We march upstairs to unwrap. The top room is a full-fledged doper's den, painted slick green with red trim, a single window bringing enlightenment. Pipes, papers, tape cassettes, carefully cornered handtooled shitboxes. We contribute to the general debilitation by spreading out Berber rugs, sheepskins, poufs--all our loot. Perhaps that was some inner precognitive response to . . . but I jump ahead. Sometimes you should and sometimes not.

Get the right knack and you are a tolba.

First things first, that's a saying the Swiss have. Where could we score some shit NOW? (This was where we came in in Marrakech.) He makes a jillion phone calls and finally locates some Honest Empire Brazilian grass! Unheard of in London! Matter of fact, our pal Gypsy has never even smoked grass, though he's a regular hash feend. Well, this cat lives in St. John's Wood, mon. We've got to take a taxi. Only cost a pound or so. (Let's see, that's $2.80 or $2.40 or something; buy two weeks food in Morocco.)

So we pile into a taxi, figuring it as sightseeing expenses, and head for St. John's Wood. My mother always said I was easily influenced.

Now we're in some other dude's place and sitting around a big pile of Brazilian grass and Gypsy is asking me through the haze whether it's a good deal or not and I have to tell him judiciously that all things considered and weighing the pros and cons and figuring the assets and liabilities and calculating the credit and debit and generally being thrown about on the horns of an Andalusian dilemma--that it's a good deal. He has bid ten pounds, which I now know to be worth $24, for a clean ounce of this firecracker and possibly even dynamite grass.

    MEMORY: A green gouda cheese of electric Moroccan hash, a veritable ingot, one hunnert grams Fahrenheit, ten bucks.

    MEMORY: One kilo of Culiacán opiated trance-inducing motherfucker loco weed, five bucks.

Now Gypsy is realizing he has forgotten his leather pouch and could I front him ten pounds and of course I could, my friend. I pull out a freshly translated wad of English doggerel and peel off ten quid. We take another taxi back to Wimbledon. This little escapade has set us back what in Morocco would pay the rent for six months and throw in two servants. Buncha fucking <u>dope addicts</u>!

        MEMORY: The Grand Sheikh of the Sufis, barefoot and ragged, effortlessly working through the marketplace.

        SEGUÉ: The Tarascan Indian in Mexico who sat under the tree outside for three days and nights, waiting to collect a debt.

    We make a few haphazard attempts to score flats the next day and run up against Queen Victoria.
    "I'm sorry," says the bloated old Russian burlie starlet. "I'll have to have some references." We offer her cash money, but she padlocks her crotch. We offer her the Milk Marketing Board, Alfred A. Knopf, and Yankee Stadium. She wavers and consults her husband, who is behind a Chinese screen.
    "I'm sorry," she says when she comes out, a little breathless. "Don't you know a Governor of the Bank of England or something?" We go out in disgust, pick up a copy of the <u>Financial Times</u>, and send her a clip of the latest gold prices.

        MEMORY: A certain episode in Morocco where we ended up being owed favors by the U.S. Consul General, Voice of America, Interpol, and the CIA.

    We return to Mirja and Gypsy's in a wet funk and they try doctoring us with hash and tobacco. We could never make it with this particular European fetish. We try, to be nice, and it makes us sick. Suddenly, there's a knock at the door! It is the Pakistani overlord come to have a word with Mr. Ruppen about the "guests."

"In thees country," he says in his sprucest Oxford, "we do not entertain guests for more than one night!"

Gypsy and Mirja look at him frogeyed.

"This is not the customary procedure, you understand," he continues. They have retired to the lower landing so we won't hear, but we creep down like the little kids peeking through the stairrails at their parents' party.

"Look, mon, we rent this place from you and that's it!" Gypsy retorts. "What do we pay you fifty-two pounds a month for?"

It goes back and forth, the Pakistani quoting his exhaustive knowledge of the "proper procedure," the Swiss standing on his currency. The Finn gets in a few licks about communal sauna baths, but nothing telling.

We make ourselves known:

"My dear fellow, if you have something to say about us, why don't you tell us directly!" Three shocked pans. This is definitely not the proper procedure. We stride haughtily down the stairs, pressing our advantage.

The landlord recovers quickly. "I was telling Mr. Ruppen that in this country we do not invite guests without first getting the approval of the landlord, and when they stay overnight that means I'm renting to four people, not two, and blah blah blah landlord talk!"

"Yes, well, what of it?"

"You must therefore blah customary procedure."

"My dear fellow, you must be putting us on!"

"This is outrageous! You cannot possibly blah blither drivel!"

"Look, man, we just differ, that's all. We just think differently from you about these things."

He thinks we're making a cut at his race, rather than his age.

"That is ridiculous, nonsense! We do not think differently! That is utter nonsense, balderdash!" He quotes six paragraphs from today's *Times* and names the last fourteen Earls of Leicester.

He finally agrees we can stay on longer, just as we decide to fuck it.

We go out with our heads immersed in steel wool.

"Let's go someplace."

We go, by taxi. Then we go somewhere else, by taxi. This whole bit is getting ridiculous and expensive. Mirja and Gypsy insist on taxis. We explain that we are fresh out of the orange squeezer. Words are said and we take a taxi again.

Inside the taxi. Facing off. We start to talk about Morocco and it goes like this:

GYPSY: Yah, mon, fucking Moe-rock-ko, you have to treat the fucking Arabs like dey is people! Is not the same as Yoo-rup, where dey are just dirt!

MIRJA: Yah, and they are so--uncultured! They have no culture, the Arabs!

ME: Are you out of your fucking minds? The Arabs invented algebra and medicine and had the greatest culture in the world!

GYPSY: Hmm.

MIRJA: Yah.

Oh, man!

Time to split, if ever time was. Bad scene.

We score loan of a car from some other friends and the next day we drive off in all directions.

Jesucristo, is this the Promised Land? Well, OK, it's nice to speak English again.

      Scene: In a restaurant. The "Dr. Watson," or something along that line. We order.

      ME: And waitress, could you please bring us some water?

      WAITRESS: I ain't got time for water!

Now, by Dog, in Morocco they'd <u>never</u> say they ain't got time for water! Simple as that! Where would we be if God said "I ain't got time for water!"?

We drive around like idjits for two days, going in ever-widening circles, completely fucked about by Western cyclic thought. We end up one day in a little village called Richmond-upon-Thames. We nab a stray hotel room and scout for flats. They are scarcer than moon dust around London. One week's rent here equals three months' rent in Morocco--and that's a tiny two-room flat versus a luxurious villa with gardens and ocean overlook!

This housing shortage is severely retarding our integration. We look at a lot of places, some nice. They want references from Buckingham Palace or at least Kensington High Street. The rents are stupendous and you can't use the garden and you have to truck through the landlady's sitting room to get to your flat. How do the English do it? The median income is only about $50 a week, and your average secretary bird makes only $35. It's that old economic blues again, the one that first assaulted us in Morocco before we got into the spiritual thing (oh, how far away that seems!).

> DREAM: I am sitting, surrounded by friends or disciples, reading a morocco leather-bound Whole Earth book. The lefthand page is black linoleum cut, the right white papyrus. I open to the section on "Stonehenge" and see a three-column illuminated picture of a rock-and-roll band.

I wake up the next morning and am struck by a thunderbolt. "Holy shit!" I cry. "Stonehenge is a rock group!!"

That day we find a flat.

>   As the pig bends
>   To lace his shoe
>   So goes the government
>   Kick his ass.

Marocalum

Protect your reputation;
Puff yourself up
   At the neighborhood cafe.
While you're at it
Enter the TV raffle
And tell an American he's
   "Groovy."
As for po' folk,
They get a separate song,
Just like always the world over.

<u>Refrain</u>:
Raise 'em poor
To make 'em standard;
Oh, it's smart to be standard
And poor!

    Lurking about like a slyboots. Penetrating the groaning abbeys of Smoketown. Prodding modern roundabouts, slit them sideways to uncover shady old plazas on the rot. See the spot where Lenin spat and Marx studied. Feel Akhnaton's muscle. Pore over old vellum. Chemical comparisons forging memory chain, recycling for ever-keener observation—don't throw away those old links! Audible "clank" when hooking up to Western level collective unconscious.

Vibrations ripple from end to end, redoubling as they radiate, psychomechanical multiplier detonating laughing bursts to shiver the grime off rusty, shriveled apparatus.

Swimming with doubledecker Royal submarine through a sea of fish faces. Remember the aquarium of the Zoco Chico: there they were dolphins and sharks, here they're guppies and fat mercury-filled tuna with mustachios. Prolific Arabian flounder swim circles and pentagrams around prolix British perch. But the perch is a plodder, by Gad, he'll muddle through somehow! Why, ask anyone who went to school with him!

We meet antiquity over a mahogany table in a domed reading room. Antiquity meets modernity when there's a bomb scare! Seems the reading room attendants are striking for higher wages, better working conditions, and bilingualism in Quechua. It is all handled very quietly, so as not to wake the neighbors. We discuss matters under Nefertiti, facing Ra.

Connect. "I'd like to make a connect call to Morocco . . ." Only connect. So says the man in the wych-elm. We discover Kew Gardens and wych-elms, redwoods, fat fig palms, weeping willow swan hollows, Tibetan berries, wild wisteria, and Chinese pagodas. If you fly your kite just right in the big green on the Twickenham road, bordering Kew, you can see the Chinese pagoda in the distance and the white Tibetan chorten just to your left. It's a man-lifter!

We walk into the green a bit more, directly onto the dragon line. That's an energy ray the Druids drew, or discovered, radiating from Glastonbury out into the cosmos. When they discovered these lines of raw energy they built their churches smack on top of them. The mother Church underwent internal surgery, however, and the center shifted from Glastonbury to Canterbury. Now they won't tell you about the dragon unless you consult the proper authorities. We make like we're going out of the green, but quick sneak under the bridge that's almost hidden in a far corner. We come upon a strange mound. A conical structure perches atop. Herbs grow up this mound that don't grow anywhere else around. It is worth investigating, but personally, it makes my hair stand on end. We hurry on out, past two huge wych-elms, and encounter the ancient palace of Henry VIII. Not Hampton Court, where all the tourists go, but Richmond Palace. Life and deathplace of Henry VII, Henry VIII, and Elizabeth I. We walk through whistling (holding our heads under our arm) and eventually emerge on Richmond Green. Shakespeare lived in the cute white house on the corner. You can't fly a kite too well in this Green, though, because the 148 tall elm trees block the wind.

We were tripping around on Richmond Green one day, one of those rare sunny days in England when everything turns to golden liquid light. We had just spent some time in the local library (where, believe it or not, they carry Sane Occultism by Dion Fortune) when we decided to go over to the bookstore and check out the latest magazines. We wound through a little seventeenth-century passerelle lined with herbalists and antique dealers, crossed the busy road, and went into W. H. Smith's, Disinfected Booksellers.

A common enough pursuit. My particular habits were to riffle through Time and Newsweek, examine Time Out (a hip guide to London), new book titles, good covers, picture books--you know, the usual shit. But for some reason, this time I was drawn to those halfassed astrology magazines. I believe in astrology, of course, but have always regarded those popular magazines as just pure ratshit. You know, "You're Aries and therefore have a big, throbbing cock." But this time, I don't know. Something just came over me.

I opened one up and checked out the horoscope for that month. Do this, don't do this, do that, watch out for a devious these, good month for romance. But then I turned to the back and found something I had never noticed before. They carry psychic ads in those fuckers. I guess I should have figured, but it surprised me. "Have your palm read by the Masked Magician." "Send your birth data to Sadie Grimpuss, 23 Edgeware Road, along with £25, and sit tight." Farther on they have classifieds. The section on "Societies" caught my eye. There was a full ad for the Theosophical Society. Now, I know about them. They're legit. An old, established, occult and philosophical society devoted to research on the Ancient Wisdom. H'rumph. Just below that ad was another, for some group I'd never heard of. The name intrigued me: The Atlanteans.

"The Atlanteans is a society with a philosophy which believes in the importance of individual thought. Within this framework we have a way of life, an understanding of the universe which acknowledges the existence of God as an Ultimate Thought."

Hmm. Is this just occult jargon, or what?

"We encourage each person to seek expression as an individual and through this seeking we find a meaning to life, a flow of thought which sweeps aside frustrations and misunderstandings and allows us to develop spiritually, mentally, and physically."

Yeah, well, who doesn't?

"We believe in an extra sense which enables us to transcend the barriers of materialism. For those who wish to step further on to the paths of metaphysics we can offer an understanding of the occult which dispenses with many of the old traditions and presents it in an acceptable way. The source of our inspiration, which comes from an esoteric plane, has guided us in this approach to the universe."

Ah! Now you're talking! Shit, if it ain't "transcending the barriers of materialism" that our alleged "counterculture" is about, then I don't know! Why had we gone to Morocco in the first place?

What really got us, though, was the name. Atlanteans. Atlantis. What true freak doesn't relate to Atlantis? Remember that incredible beach in Tangier, the one with the Phoenician ruins? Well, Plato mentions that as the tip of Atlantis. The Caves of Hercules. Things were connecting. And those Berbers. Their legends put them as originating in Atlantis, migrating to "North Africa" when the mighty island continent got too big for its bridges, after the invention and subsequent misuse of the fabulous "firestone." What we now call a "laser." Is there any wonder Atlantean souls are now again striving to reincarnate? They want to pay their bill. Is there any wonder us American blown-head types are attracted to Morocco and other ancient music? Connecting with the Dealer of It All. In Morocco we had done our pure research; now came Developmental Engineering.

First Atlantean meeting. In a friendly house surrounded by cheek-brushing fruit trees who acknowledge our right to be here.

We expect, no doubt, a starry headdress, a copper cuirass, delicately juggled lightning bolts, a deep soulful look we must ache to penetrate, a reading of the Law. Bah! Comic book backlash! Far out Moroccans had looked far out wise or not. We hadn't realized a wise man could just be <u>normal</u>. Now I think of it, I believe that fellow Jesus was just <u>a plain</u>, simple dude.

No hoods, no glassy eyes, no secret smiles, and no flies on the Atlanteans. Good vibes straightaway. We check out the literature:

"Atlantean Views On Life Today." Nineteen important lectures including: Know Thyself, Class Structure, Murder, Justice and Social Laws, Sex, How One Should Live One's Life.

"Life Outside The Physical Body, And Colour." Covering:

Animal Evolution, Intelligence and Reincarnation, The Astral Planes, Guides and Controls, Auras and Auric Colours, Colour, Cosmic Law, Sleep State, The Occult Sciences.

"Earth Past and Future and Her Planetary Neighbours." Which tells of the beginning of the Earth, the Significance of the Sun, The Moon, Time and Space, The Planets and Flying Saucers, The Future and Comments on Astrology.

"Jesus, the Prophets, and God." Jesus Christ, His Life and Work, The Bible, The Revelations, Prayer and Religion in General, God, The Ultimate.

"Cosmic Law and the World Today." The Population Explosion, Cosmic Law, Psychic Ramifications of Radiation, Thought Waves and the Solar System, The Ever-Expanding Universe, The Semitic Race, The Esoteric Significance of England, France, America, Russia, China, India, and South Africa, The Fall of This Planet.

"Atlantis--Past and To Come." Historical, occult and scientific viewpoints concerning legendary Atlantis. Contributors include Helio-Arcanophus, the High Priest of the Sun in Atlantis.

"Spirit Evolution." The Spirits of the Elements, the Occult Effects of Drug Taking, the Positive and Negative Aspects of Creation, the Four Horsemen of the Apocalypse, Power Centers, and other lectures for the advanced student.

Woof. Scientific Sufis. Here's where Morocco left off. They've got the personality thing down, but they still work with foot lathes. That's cool, that's _great_, but--it's not what's happening! Arabia had its day back in the thirteenth century, results available for introspection. But now is the future. Underpinned by Atlantis and pasts remoter. Nourished by drawing from the deep well of Ageless Wisdom. Now. The Age of the Water Carrier. And besides, they speak English!

At this moment, puncto, the folk carrying the occult water are just plain folk. They make no special claims. They ask no special recognition. They just do their plain, incredible folk thing.

> FLASH: The Zoco Chico in Tangier. We emerge from a vein flowing into the Casbah's throbbing heart. A commotion asserts itself at the right

ventricle and we mosey on over to feel the beat.

Bet you didn't know the heart is ringed by cafes! Each table and chair vivified by waving, craning ganglia plotting a corner on the cholesterol market. Now they are antibodied on this embolism up at the right ventricle, which seems to be making the heartbeat very rapid. We do some craning and waving ourselves, and see that this is no ordinary coronary. Rather mere along esoteric valves: heart and soul, the goodness of your heart--you know, like that. We see ten whirling dancing dervishes, twitching to the rhythm of a skin drum. They dance endlessly. By means of certain sounds, or signals less perceivable, they weave their dance among themselves.

Two whirl violently for fully fifteen centuries, then subside to mere foot shuffling while two more take up the eerie quickbeat. The drummer throws bolts of lightning out to selected spectators.

These dancers are old men. None is below sixty! Yet they have been dancing for two solid days and will go on until they drop. It is Mohammed's birthday. But, ah!--the prejudice of the authority-loving Occidental. For in Arabic, "Mohammed" also means "every man."

There is no God but Allah, and Mohammed is his Prophet. <u>La ilaha il'Allah oo M'hamd urrasululah!</u> A search for <u>Sufis in W. H. Smith's?</u> Why not? Even so-called wise men used to think tea was rare and only found in certain remote places.

We walk into the meeting and see friends we have missed for lifetimes. A direct hit on the pineal. A game is in progress, directed at those who just inquire and those who harbor lurking skepticism. This game is "Psychometry." You take an object and read its vibrations. Three mediums (media?) sit up front, on the barrelhead, and fondle keys and lockets. For us, the game was twofold: we had never seen psychometry (except what all of us practice every day, like when you enter a room and it feels creepy) and we had this lesson to learn about ordinary-looking

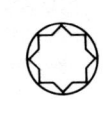

people. I mean, one of these far out medium dudes looked like the guy who brushes his teeth on the Arm and Hammer Baking Soda box. Mohammed means "every man." The Christ in the heart. I salute the God within. That was _our_ hangup about long hair and freakiness. It served its purpose and now is headed for sewage treatment. It doesn't matter: these are friends.

Just like looking at Moroccans and knowing that they collectively were part of our life trip. Same with the Atlanteans. We just knew. (They even knew better than we did.) A connection made on a deeper level than just intellect, or emotion. Who knows what to say about it? It's part of the incredible Art of it all.

So they did their number on the trinkets. "I see a yew tree. Beyond it is a broad meadow. Green--very lush. Someone is walking in the meadow . . . who seems to be losing his way. He's not sure. He is heading for the rough ground at the outskirts of the meadow, not sticking to the grassy plain. . . . I get a flash of Egypt. I--I . . . that's all."

A band of highly sensitive magnetic tape unwinds on my spinal spindle, leaving a print-through of skepticism recorded some ten years earlier. Or, it's like when you're macrobiotic you get twinges of your previous diseases, as the brown rice cleanses your system completely. I remember Houdini's trip with Rahman Bey, the Hindu Yogi who stopped his heartbeat to the satisfaction of the proverbial "committee of doctors." Houdini thought and thought and consulted his old Thurston books, and came up with a perfect replica. But did that prove it was a trick, or just that it _could_ be faked? I mean, nowadays you have electronic alpha-wave control to allegedly duplicate Zen meditation, but that doesn't prove meditation was done with electromagnets hidden in the lotus roots. It's the new science of bionics. Approximately this set of inter-synaptic relays tripped off in my head.

A thin, nervous-looking man walked up to the barrelhead and claimed his bauble.

"Thank you very much," he said earnestly. "That really makes a lot of sense to me. Thank you."

A lot of words went down and that meeting ended. The words were just regular. But the reality was something incredible. It was like a Morocco reality. I know you understand that by now. That's the connection here. It's all bound up in all the possible places. Total experience (fucking waterbed bourgie cliché by now). IT!

I remember the mineral baths in Tiberias. Natural hot springs. You could swim for half an hour, sleep for an hour, and then hit the cool mountain air! IT! You take a sauna bath, hot rocks steaming their fool heads off, then roll naked in the new snow!

It was like a warm, living wind had swept through our lives, cleansing the furniture in our minds and impregnating lemon oil love wisdom. Words, words, words.

> THREAD: Sitting on the streetedge table of the CTM cafe. Right on the Jamaa el-F'na. Not fifty yards away the snake charmers charm snakes and the healers they heal. I sip mint tea. Two small boys come up and ask me for sugar. I have only one cube and I give it to one of them. The other grabs for it. A full-fledged fight erupts. It continues about three seconds, until an ordinary-looking Arab (is there one?) appears from nowhere. He gently lays his hands on each boy's head. The fight stops instantly. All three disperse.

A week of yattering, then another Atlantean convex.
Quotable quotes: "This is fundamentally a teaching society."
We discuss healing and human auras, everyone learning according to his capacity and readiness. "If you break a bone, go to an osteopath; if you break something deeper, go to a psychiatrist or a psychic." They did a demonstration, using a gimp who volunteered. I thought of Oral Roberts and Billy James Hargis, where the dude throws away his crutches and gives

his polo ponies to the Church, but nothing like that happened. (They stressed that the conditions were far from ideal.) They did genuine healing sessions before each meeting. Any questions?

"Yeah," I said. "I got a question."

"What is it?"

"Well, it seems to me that it's . . . heavy to put your aura in someone else's hands. I mean, how do we know what you're doing with it? How do we really know?"

Whoops! That ol' lurking science smell.

The answer comes through a warm, enigmatic smile: "You just have to go by the feelings you get from us. There aren't any sort of credentials for this sort of thing." Can you imagine? Here's Arm and Hammer telling me to pick up on the vibes! And he was right!

It's fair enough, I reflected. I had to admit that I got extremely good vibes from all of them so far. They seemed to always speak exactly in accord with one's fitness to understand. That struck me as being almost a union rule for a wise man. Eliminate communication problems. I remember those looks we got in Morocco from the desert sages, the watersellers and that incredible old man with his donkey who said: "You have much and want more. I have nothing and want nothing."

All this guru shit us kids go through nowadays! The fucking teachers are right here, right around us, all the time! It just takes a sense of forward energy--grooving. Make a vow to learn from experience--even the little, "insignificant" ones. It's like someone hypnotized you to be constantly stoned without any smoke. When you understand that each event, object, or person is just a symbol for inner, creative forces . . . well, then! There's no telling what might happen! This is a higher correspondence of what we felt on the boat: that there's more to . . . uh . . . "things" than Walter Cronkite or Marx or even our Moms tell us. On the boat we envisioned a search for data. The facts. Now we're involved in transmuting this to a search for meaning. How the trick is done.

When you find a scrap of paper on the street with your phone number on it, you can dismiss it as "just" a coincidence-- or you can regard it as meaningful! This is why Orientals have produced no "science." They've been out picking up scraps of paper off the floor of the Diogenes Club!

OK. Groovy. So what? So this: the Atlanteans are into

healing. That's their trip. That's how they use the fruits of the mystic bon-bon tree. That's what keeps it from being a North Beach ego trip. Direct use of the mind's energy. It's not "Get your head together so you can snow the next butt-twitch chick and ram the energy of Mars up her Venus honeypot." It's that old saw: "In all superstition, wise men follow fools." Accepting the vows of occultism (self-imposed) means you recognize that you are an agent of evolution. We are evolution, if we would only see it. The Power can be contacted by desire to cooperate. The method of contact is meditation, or you name it.

Contact with a Master: the Atlanteans operated by some mysterious psycho-lube works. At every meeting a new bolt of our personalities was tightened, a new shot of grease applied. We didn't know fuck about it, except that it was happening and that Morocco had been a necessary tune-up. The actual contact is helpful. They say that when the student is ready the master appears. Possibly the necessary yeast can be evolved from one's own inner being, but that is highly improbable without a recipe.

How do you really know? You just know. You know? That's the whole bleedin' trip, right there. You just plain fucking know. Womens' intuition. In ancient Atlantis they knew--and they blew it. This is what I mean by Service. This is what I mean by California. Dig it--the Berbers were blown back to the Stone Age. They had that fucking firestone. All clairvoyant investigation reaffirms it. The legends allude to it. We're at the point now where Eastern and Western VOOF! Come together! The new root race. The Seventh Ray. (But remember, Hitler was a mystic, too.)

Atlantis died like Krypton, by not listening to its wise men. Like Krypton, Atlantis sent out some super men, who've just lately come out on to this planet where they are so sorely needed. You saw their disciples behind the San Francisco Trips Festival, at Golden Gate Park every Sunday, at political rallies, conventions, test-driving Corvairs, in the underground newspapers. They're still around, I believe, doing what the times demand, and asking no special favors. They know. Some of them are doing religious trips, some not. Some of them have long hair, some not. Some are travelers, some sedentary. Some are clerks, some tradesmen, some artists, some think-tankers. Doing what's right. Paying the long-due bill. All tuned in to the facts of our present evolution. All working by the pattern of things to come. Knowers. Atlanteans, Lemurians, professional pool hustlers.

Engineering on the inside Reality. Joyce once said he was the greatest engineer in the world. Scientific as the next man (who happens to hail from the Cameroons and . . .) (who happens to hail from Atlantis and . . .).

I once met a kid who had heard about a power box. He and his friend went off to Morocco to find it. They knew it was there somewhere. They finally met up with an old Berber mountaineer and they kept pestering him about the box so persistently that he finally gave up, took them back to his tighremt, ran upstairs, and gave it to them. The kid opened the box and saw--everything!

"I saw colors that I just can't describe to you--like nothing I'd ever seen. I saw the past and the future. I saw Life and Death and Kings and Slaves and espionage and counter-espionage. I saw sun domes and earthquakes and maple sugar time up north. I saw Pluto and Sirius, the Dog Star. I tell you--I saw everything!"

He and his friend took the box back home and the kid got more and more attached to it. It got so he couldn't bear to be away from that box. He was extremely afraid that someone would try to steal it from him. He thought about the box constantly. Finally, his friend couldn't stand it anymore. He pilfered the box in the dead of night and buried it in the Sahara. The kid was going there to find it when we met.

Round trip: Morocco to England and points west via Atlantis. The way is trodden, tramping down suspicious herbal paths now declared illegal once used to energize teleport machines in the ancient kingdom. The stupendous amount of energy in a little seed. Nature's computer and powerhouse. Listen to the "Rite of Spring." Planted behind closed doors to avoid complications, later brought into the open to grow into a scattershot network of interlocking branches, somewhat like a banyan tree, under which one could live in an artistic manner. Now, this minute, replanted (it is periodical, not perennial) and sending a long sinuous taproot down, down the wormways of time. A bolt of ancient mindsap works through capillary action. Since we're dealing with a distance of over ten thousand years, it wasn't a bad idea to stop off in the Middle Ages for recharging. And that is what we did.

VI

WHOLE EARTH LIBERATION FRONT

Sitting at the Source

Birdsong taps out codewords
To break the lock on the "Football"
(That nuclear briefcase
Never far from Nixon's finger tip).
We don't need recording, playback and analysis machines:
Only a simultaneous interpreter.

The prana circulates. The hair on the androids is getting good
in back and it works out that the Beatles were just a big hype.
Hip was roasted on a spittle--oh, so long ago. Are we left with
a dribbling mess, or the dawn of Time's new day?
    The weight of evidence is--heavy. Even engineers won't deny

that this is the Age of Aq. They refer it to another department. The thoughtform is upon us, whether you call it trinitro energy nuggets, unfoldment of the soul, or self-determination. Now must be developed the physical encasement.

At this moment the movement is upon the land. Pure food, wind harnesses, sun heat day or night--clean technology, thunk up by nuclear babies. Next breath's problems will be of a different order entirely. The new atomic bomb lies between the eyebrows.

Do you see? It all synthesizes. Stand back from the mad mirror of now and sense NOW. Go back, back beyond the written word, the spoken speech, the thought thought. Go back before the deluges, back even before the Ages of the Arcane. Grok the rhythm, in and outweave in the light. Know the Fact, which no one denies but few accept: the fact of evolution.

So is it God, or the Central Energy, or the Ultimate Abstraction? Who cares! At a certain point in the life of an organism--an individual, a group, a people, a race--there comes a decision to throw all forces onto the side of evolution. At this point you enter the Path.

For instance. The mystic acid visions are now firmly ground up in the mortar of our group soul. Riflefire response proves they, too, are Maya--illusion. Nevertheless, they goose us farther up the spiral. We now tread upon that former work. In the central spindle of our innermost cortex we know that all men are one. We accept the fact of periodicity ("Going through changes"). The next lesson is the progressive development of everything--remember, everything is conscious. Everything is Life. Evolution. How <u>did</u> that rock become that one-celled animal, anyway?

Behind every object or event lies a thought. Moreover, there lies a connection to all other men, events, and thoughts. This crosslegged Moroccan hashish eater I keep for good luck came from the thoughts of a woodcarver (who came from the thoughts of his parents), combined with the thoughts of the whittlin' knifemaker, from the ecology of the Marrakech argan forest (and thence from the first seed ever sown) all back, back, back to the first man. And thus to the Ultimate Thought.

Can you see how the problems of humanity might have their roots in some forgotten triviality of millenia past (before the flood?) and how even the most stoned brilliant solutions we dream up are nothing but fluff without a clue to the source and the rhythm?

Example. Recently there was a top-secret conference at the Menninger Foundation. Bunch of super-straight Ph.D's and M.D.'s all interested in parapsychology. Keynote address given by a well-known psychic who blew the mind of an old harrumpher in the audience by reading it. For a few days the docs amused themselves with Zener card tricks. But then. . . . Up stood Rolling Thunder, chief medicine man for the Shoshone tribe. He had spent most of the time in the woods. He said he was getting the feel of the conferees and had found much goodwill. How would you like to see a healing, he asked.

Would we! they answered.

There was a medical student there who had injured his leg in a soccer match. He had an infected six-inch gash in it. About thirty M.D.'s looked at it and said, yes, it is infected. The student said it was very painful.

Rolling Thunder put the kid onto a table and left the room. He returned wearing an old hat and carrying a battered suitcase. He began to carefully question the boy about his motives for being healed.

At first, the kid said he just wanted to be healed because it hurt and he didn't like hurting. Rolling Thunder gently led him into exploring his real purposes in life, and the student eventually saw that he wanted to be healed so he could better serve his fellow man.

At this point, Rolling Thunder opened the suitcase. He took out an eagle's wing and a bowl of raw meat. He put the bowl of meat at the boy's feet, and began to chant. He began passing the eagle's wing over the boy's "aura."

After this "aural massage," he took a pipe out of the case, lit it, puffed, and offered prayers to the East, West, South, and North, to the Sun Father above and the Earth Mother below. He then offered the pipe to the young man, who puffed gingerly. Rolling Thunder prayed.

The medicine man then smelled the wound. He hissed and then yowled like a wolf. He chirped. He took a mouthful of clear water from a bowl and put his mouth onto the wound. He spit out a mouthful of yellowed water ("I swear he didn't break the skin!"), got sick, and vomited. He took another mouthful of clear water and repeated the operation twice more, vomiting.

By this time the boy was smiling.

Rolling Thunder passed the eagle's wing over the student's body, then shook it at the raw meat.

The boy shouted, "I'm healed! I'm healed!"

Twenty M.D.'s leaped from their seats onto the stage and examined the boy. They could find no break in the skin and the kid said he felt no pain. There was a small scab.

When asked later what they thought of the whole thing, the M.D.'s replied in wonder: "We don't think. We saw."

Now, this is all very beautiful. But here's the hitch: all the M.D.'s and Ph.D.'s are doing their research under bulletbrain grants. The grantors don't know they're doing ESP work. They think they're just doing regular therapeutic research. Therefore, so as not to lose their grants, the scientists want to keep the results of this conference secret.

But, now! Isn't this how Atlantis perished? Secret teachings for sale to the blackest bidder! Isn't this how we got the atomic bomb? When they asked Einstein, "Hey, couldn't you use this here relativity to make a bomb?" he said, "No, impossible, beat it!" Linus Pauling is still trying to atone for that one. The road to extinction is paved with wiseacres. Science is too vital to be left to the scientists.

This is that neutron bomb they've been talking about for years, the one that zaps people but leaves the buildings standing. This is the power to scramble men's minds or suck life's blood. We must keep it out of the wrong claws. This is why the doctrines have been secretly held in custody of esoteric groups for so long. But now is the time for revelation, and now we--the people--have the chance to do the thing or get shoveled under. It's in the open now. They are doing ESP experiments from the moon--classified information. WE CANNOT LET IT HAPPEN AGAIN!!

Everyone knows this is the crucial juncture in evolution. The Earth functions as a whole system. This is the last civilization because it is unbounded. The powers of the mind are becoming recognized planetwide. The head center of humanity is being opened. The heart center must direct it wisely with love.

I'm not going to leave it at a sappy platitude. There is a concrete hunk of learnin' that has to be learned to handle this situation. It's all out front available, in books, from esoteric groups and in many, many forms. But it's the kind of knowledge that can't be just absorbed into the cranial sponge. It must be meditated, cogitated and <u>lived</u>. Habits must be broken. Adaptation must begin.

> Troupers of the People,
> We learn by Arabia's
>   biting, blinding sands
> That the proper laws in harness
> Will catapult us
> Into the crossbow seat.
>
> To keep in proper tune
> Learnt from a <u>melhoun</u>
> We must expect--
> Nay, <u>insist</u>--
> On our right to be
> Change's victim
> The next time round.

Can't you hear them Yugas grindin'? They make that ancient music.

The synthesis is upon us and it takes a synthetic grasp to grasp it. It's a new elliptical orbit ballgame. One thing the bomb did for us, it organized our minds. If it hadn't been for pollution we wouldn't have thought about whole systems and survival. Now we're there. That's the objective work to be done. But let's don't slip: I saw an ad the other day for Silva Mind Control, Inc. You can regard that as a hot tip for the stock market or a new character in the world dance.

They say the great feature of the Piscean Age was obedience to authority. The New Age will be characterized by joy and ceremony. Thus one last thought, from the Secret Doctrine. The Lord Buddha has said that "we must not believe in a thing said merely because it is said; nor traditions because they have been handed down from antiquity; nor rumors, as such; nor writings by sages, because sages wrote them; nor fancies that we may suspect to have been inspired in us by a Deva; nor from inferences drawn from some haphazard assumption we may have made; nor because of what seems an analogical necessity; nor on the mere authority of our teachers or masters. But we are to believe when the writing, doctrine, or saying is corroborated by our own reason and consciousness. 'For this,' says he in concluding, 'I taught you not to believe merely because you have heard, but when you believed of your consciousness, then to act accordingly and abundantly.'"

APPENDIX

1 Hashish Heebie-Jeebies: A Magic Lesson

Come on over to the Walled Garden some time, get stoned, and I'll show you some magic. I don't mean I'll say magic things (though I might), and I may not even put on a robe (though watch it if I wear a vest). But I will show you a method of hypnotism against one's will (if that's the way you want it; it works even better if you play along). If we're in expansive moods--and the dope is good--we may discover a key or a pry to the crack between the worlds. Or we might even find some of that cold roast pork left!
   Here is straight skinny: I've been doing sleight-of-hand magic for years, and one thing I've learned is that people only see what they want to see, or what they expect to see. Not what is really there.
   Let me give you an example. I do a routine with four red sponge balls, about the size of golf balls, or universes. I hold one ball in my right hand, between the index and third fingers. I slowly, ever so slowly, place this ball into the center of my left palm. Still gripping it in the right fingers, I close my left fingers around the ball. I slowly slide my right fingers out--empty--and raise my closed left hand high. I make a crumpling motion with the left hand, open it slowly, and--the sponge ball has vanished!
   I show both hands empty and take a bow. Then I reach into empty space and pluck the ball out of thin air! I put it into my other hand, close the hand for a moment, and reopen it to show-- two balls! I take the two balls, put them into the other hand, close it briefly, and reopen it with--three balls! I take the three, put them into the other hand and emerge with four! Bows.
   There's always a cheeky aspirant who has to know more, out

of scientific curiosity. A friend of mine, Jani, calls it "being the dope." The dope gets invited up to sit in a special chair. He's now facing the audience. I stand at his left, with my left side to the audience. First you can be the dope, then the audience.

As the dope you see this: Right in front of your very nose, I vanish the four balls entirely, one at a time. I take a ball, put it into my left hand, tap the left hand with the right ("Give a magic tap . . .") and the ball vanishes. Completely. I show both hands completely empty, both sides, short sleeves. The audience titters, but you are completely astounded. This is repeated four times. By the fourth time, you--the dope--are absolutely stonkered! A sneaking, uncomfortable mystification: perhaps there _is_ something to this magic business, after all. I mean, there's _no_ other ready explanation!

As the audience, you see this: behind the scenes. Instead of putting the sponge ball into my left hand, I actually "thumb palm" it in the right. While the dope thinks I'm "tapping the left hand with the right," I actually _throw the ball over his head!_ The ball is released above his eye level, and he suspects nothing. I tell you, I've done this thousands of times and it works on everyone from kindergarten kids to German scientists. (As a matter of fact, the more educated the dope is the better it seems to work!)

You understand how "Morocco" is a symbol of certain inner forces. Some High Goblin compels us to go, to seek--IT! In a microcosmic moment, this magic routine symbolizes our quest, while emphasizing certain facts or illusions of conditioning which we all contend with. Or must be content with.

Take the dope. He sees a certain phenomenon and calls it magical. He is partly right and partly ignorant.

Take the audience. They see the same phenomenon and call it flummery. They are partly right and partly ignorant, too.

Take the magician. He knows the secret and knows how to do the trick so it teaches a lesson about hypnotism. He is tuned in to the _whole situation._ But he is part of the situation nevertheless.

"Not only don't we have any solutions, we're part of the problem!"

The dope is like someone who has had a "mystical experience." He is unwilling to go behind the scenes. This, in my opinion, is excellent to a certain point, for surely the appreciation of the <u>art</u> of Creation is a giant step to knowledge. And, it's fun!

The audience is like someone who's a science head. He knows nothing of the magic of life, simply because he sits in the wrong chair. Naturally, he laughs at the open-mouthed wonder of the mystic.

The magician is like the Sufi, the man of knowledge. He simply <u>knows</u>--through experience--and tries to make the <u>whole situation</u> meaningful to dope and audience alike, according <u>to their</u> readiness to learn. He learns too, by doing <u>his</u> best. Artist and scientist merge. For the next act, C. P. Snow stands on his head.

The starting point is the mind-set. You think you're going to see something--and you do. Even if you <u>determine</u> to glue your eyes on the quickness of the hand--it don't <u>matter</u>. That's part of the trick. You get hypnotized against your will because you <u>don't know what your will is</u>! This ain't no lightweight universe we're stuck in, friends! Hypnotism is everywhere. "You talk 'em to sleep," is the way my butcher-dentist from Ohio puts it.

And so Morocco and Atlantis: these are the invisible magicians. This is the <u>real</u> magic. They try to talk us to sleep in school, on TV, and under-the-ground. All in the guise of enlightenment. Despite all that antagonism, somehow we still get tuned in. There are forces afoot, Watson! Each of us practices in front of his own mirror. Sometimes you get so good you even fool yourself.

Now, there are all sorts of magicians. If you want a taste (and not a bad chopped-steak lunch, either) go down to the Dixie Hotel on 42nd Street in New York City some noon. They keep a special table reserved, complete with felt pad and a new deck of cards. It's called the Dixie Magic Table. All the magicians in town gather there for lunch, absorbing and dispensing secrets like farmers sowing broadside to earthworms. If you're really into it, you can get a membership card (mine is number 212, signed by Kuda Bux and Peter Pit--a real collector's item). But mainly, dig on the magic.

There's a bald guy named Dave, for instance. By day he's an eye doctor. But at lunchtime and on weekends he's the president of the New York Ring of magicians. He carries an entire thirty-minute show around with him in one of those little Kodak film cans! Specializes in miniature magic. Microscopic art, microcosmic science.

There's a fantastic old Pakistani, Kuda Bux. You might have seen him on "You Asked For It." His trip is "sightless vision." The riff is this. You can blindfold him to your satisfaction, put dough in his eyes, wrap them with black felt--anything. Don't matter. While blindfolded, Kuda Bux has driven a race car, read sealed messages, flown and landed a plane on a narrow Himalayan pass! At the Dixie he does some incredible card effects. He vows to take his blindfold secret down with him. Inscrutable Pakistani vision. Is there a trick to it? Even Western scientific magicians don't know for certain. Maybe he does it by allegory?

Well, there are dove magicians and coin magicians, illusionists, and masked rapscallions. High magicians and low jugglers, cups and balls, and the old shell game. If the Dixie fans a spark, keep your Saturdays open. You'll want to visit Lou Tannen's.

It's right near the N.Y. Public Library. Saturday is the day of informal convocation of the top of the top, the high mackaroos of magic. Tannen sells tricks to them. If you're lucky you'll go on a day when Harry Lorayne's there.

This brings it all back home. Harry Lorayne . . . you may recognize the name. He's the dude who often stares out at you from the back page of the Sunday supplements. His third eye radiates concentric circles as he announces: "I CAN GIVE YOU A TAPE RECORDER MEMORY OVERNIGHT!" You've seen the dude.

Harry Lorayne is one of the pioneers of Western-style mind control. He also happens to be the best sleight-of-hand magician I've ever seen, and just about all the New York magicians (a jealous lot) agree. When he shows his tricks all the jabbering stops. If you've ever thought "Wow, that motherfucker must have used mass hypnosis," Harry Lorayne's your man. He did close-up card magic for thirty years, and has now graduated to incredible memory acts and executive mind training. He goes to a convention with seventeen hundred delegates, meets everyone once, and memorizes their names. You can buy his memory system for a couple of bucks. I once did. It took about two weeks to get through slowly, and when I was done I memorized the entire Russian Constitution, 164 articles, in order, for a college exam!

This cat Lorayne knows his shit. His hands are very small, too small to palm a card properly. He makes up for it by--you guessed it--mass hypnosis! He is so fucking fascinating that you don't dare take your eyes off his face! Of course, this doesn't occur to you until years later. I knew him in 1964.

One day he had just blown my mind out with an "impossible" card trick and he mentioned that he was into fancy number riffs. He wanted to write a book on speed mathematics. I happened to know a trick to multiply by eleven, and he dug it. In return, he tuned me into some of his number investigations, which form the basis of his memory system.

Basically, the trip is this. Each digit--one through zero--corresponds to one of the ten consonant sounds in the English language. Let's see, um, that's: "t" or "d," "n," "m," "r," "l," "s" or "sh," "f" or "v," "b" or "p," and "z." The "or" ones handle the voiced and unvoiced consonants. Don't worry about it; just a philologists's pride. The point is that each number has its letter equivalent. So what's the big deal? I can almost hear you ask. Who cares? But I tell you, this is the key to all things.

The way Harry Lorayne works it, it's just a memory aid. You can apply this trick to anything--a shopping list, a constitution, secret information, the serial number on a dollar bill--and memorize it. This is the symbol of our modern educational system, which is mainly memory training and operant conditioning. You remember a bunch of useless garbage, puke it back, and Right On! Who the hell cares! On this level, it's all blood pudding. But the way Israel Baal Shem Tov worked it--ah! Now, he took this trick and put the Bible to it. Perhaps you've heard of the Kabbalah? What it is, friends, is a secret code where the letters correspond to numbers. How about that? Some elevated dudes say you can't understand the Bible, or any of the ancient religious documents, without seeing the cipher for the plaintext.

And the way Jalaluddin Rumi worked it--Praise Allah! For the Sufis are philologists before all, trippers-out on the hidden meanings in words and events, and they claim to possess the real Qabalah, even before it got spelt with a "k." They say you cannot truly understand the Koran ("Qu'ran") without enciphering the Arabic into Qabalistic language and then comparing. In other words, two words that appear to have no special connection, when translated into Qabalese might have the same numerical sumtotal. This indicates a hidden connection, which is left to the meditative student to work out on the intuitive level. Now yer talkin' about who the hell cares!

Now, all this is just tricks if it ain't applied in daily

life. Until all happenings are moved off the plane of buttfucking and onto the plane of joyful ceremony, we'll still be in Vietnam. If you're a romantic you can think of yourself as a secret agent of evolution, going about engineering coups to overthrow the loveless dictatorship of your lower mind. The number game is a game if it's just a game, but if it's real, it's dynamite! Energy follows thought.

Maybe Harry Lorayne was an Arab in his last incarnation?

2   The Airwaves Belong to the People: A Music Lesson

Five o'clock in the morning. Jamaa el-F'na. It is deserted. The sun radiates peach-colored love through a dip in the blue-white Atlas peaks, picked up and transmitted by dark green palms in the surrounding forest and thrown like a shawl over cool shoulders onto the salmon-pink ramparts of Marrakech.
   A solitary Berber in a plain brown djellaba shuffles out of the dank dark of the Casbah into the huge silent square. He sits crosslegged in the exact center of the plaza, and waits.
   A golden bell of sunlight sounds silently off the minaret of the Koutoubia mosque, cueing in a high-tension whine that splits the air like the sound of howling wolves:
   "ALLAHU AQBAR--ALLAHU AQBAR."
   The Berber hears the muezzin's signal and takes a small silver flute from his robe. "ALLAHU AQBAR--GOD IS GREAT." The Berber begins to play, a clear liquid note. The sun's eye peers through the golden window.
   "ASHADU ANNA LA ILAHA IL'ALLAH--I TESTIFY THERE IS NO GOD BUT GOD--THERE IS NO GOD BUT GOD."
   The lone flutist begins a slow rhapsody to the morning, his prayer. The Casbah is awakening, the muezzin is calling the people to prayer, his music.
   The muezzin turns to the north: "ASHADU ANNA M'HAMED URRASULULAH--I TESTIFY THAT MOHAMMED IS THE PROPHET OF GOD--COME TO PRAYER--COME TO PRAYER."
   The flute picks up--how can words describe music? The flute picks up, a quicker beat. The sun is up now, the blazing desert sun gently softened by the rugged Atlas mountains.

The medina glows orange gold in the morning light. The flutist touches an orange-gold note.

The muezzin turns to the west, where the reflected light is equally wondrous: "HAJJU 'ALA'S-SALAT--SALAAAAAAAAT--COME TO SALVATION--COME TO SALVAAAAAAAASHUN."

A small Arab boy in knickers and a tunic pads barefoot out of a corner of the Casbah. He sports a tambourine. He joins the flutist in the center of the square, solemnly shaking his jangly instrument every eight beats.

Wild dogs outside the ramparts of the walled city begin to wail. The first cock crows, then another, and another. In a twinkling this sleeping fortress has become an Oriental symphony. The day's contingent of adventure seekers begins to trickle onto the giant square, the Meeting Place of the Dead, truants from their early prayers. They join the two musicians in the center. One has a tom-tom, another beats two sticks. A third plays a Jew's harp, and a fourth plays an oud--a one-string lute fashioned from a turtle shell.

The muezzin repeats his singsong call: "ALLAHU AQBAR--GOD IS GREAT--LA ILAHA IL'ALLAH OO M'HAMD URRASULULAH--HAJJU 'ALA'S-SALAT--SALAAAAAAAAT."

As the sun ultimately emerges on Marrakech the music of the muezzin completes a rainbow arc that has flashed westward at a thousand miles an hour. In Algiers we heard: ALLAHU AQBAR--GOD IS GREAT. In Tripoli, we heard: ALLAHU AQBAR--ALLAHU AQBAR. In Cairo, in Riyadh, in Damascus, in Sana, in Mecca, in Isfahan, in Qandahar, in Samarkand, in Karachi, in Rangoon, Djakarta, and Kuala Lumpur we can trace the call to prayer--which began in Oriental Java with the earliest sunrise--anointing the new day: ALLAHU AQBAR--ALLAHU AQBAR--GOD IS GREAT--GOD IS GREAT.

Marrakech is fully conscious of its rank as rear admiral of the new day and funerary herald of the old. The wondrous festival is played with full regalia, and thus the daily life of the people revolves around the carnival of the Jamaa el-F'na. This is "al-Aksa al-Maghrib": the land farthest west, the land of nightfall. A harmonic chord with California, our new Atlantis.

The players in the center of the square have done with their orisons. The Jamaa is filling steadily now, about equally with musicians and sweetmeat sellers. Morocco is up early. The first hash cookie salesman sidles up to the first customer. The first tarot reader blows the first roadblocked mind. Music resumes, this time an intricate cross rhythm, an Arabian morning raga. The lute trills high as the snake charmers arrive.

The Sufi says: "Music and singing do not produce in the heart that which is not in it. [There are] those who hear the spiritual meaning and those who hear the material sound." He goes on: "There are good and evil results in each case. Listening to sweet sounds produces an effervescence of the substance molded in man: true, if the substance be true, false, if the substance be false. When the stuff of man's temperament is evil, that which he hears will be evil, too."

"Oh, Allah," prays the Sufi sage in the marketplace this marvelous morning, "let us see things as they are."

>
> Topologically speaking,
> We'd better learn to change
> Drumheads to doughnuts
> Than vice-versa.
> (And to somehow
> Eliminate!
> Those little biting bugs.)

Someone brings the flute player his breakfast: halvah made from sesame seeds, honey, almond paste, and rose water. He drinks the "tea of aouqat," made from white and black benjoin, resin of elemi, wood of lilac, coriander, incense of oliban, and myrrh.

The Casbah's heartbeat is so strong that it wakes us up in our walled garden, clear across the medina. We hear drums and flutes.

"Music, moody food of us that trade in love."

We are awake now, and just fairly together. We fry up a mess o' grits over our Butagaz. The eggs sizzle like love in search of a word. Outside the wall we hear a sound something like high voltage mosquitoes, accompanied by drums and lutes and a lot of just plain yelling. We peer outside the heavy door to see a clot of singing, smiling folk, all dressed in white, waving banners and beating tom-toms, tambourines, and tablas.

I quickly phone the public library. "What's it mean when a bunch of Arabs are yelling and dancing and waving banners and beating tom-toms and singing like mosquitoes?"

"Just a moment, please. I'll connect you with the Arab lady."

Pause.

"Hello?"

"Hello."

"Is this the gentleman who wanted to know about the Arabs?"

"Yes."

"Well, they're going to Mecca, asshole!"

Dhun-Nun the Egyptian says: "Listening is a divine influence which stirs the heart to see Allah; those who listen to it spiritually attain to Allah, and those who listen to it sensually fall into heresy."

Al Shibley, your Square Deal Sufi, says: "Listening to music is outwardly a temptation and inwardly an admonition."

Technically speaking, Arab music is the mirror image of our Western item. It reads from right to left. The Arab's right cross seems to be our left jab. Where we ascend into the heady expansive atmosphere, the Arab gets down to the bare wet root.

In geopolitical blither, Arab music is a mixture of the Western steady beat, the African tom-tom, intricate Oriental graces, and the ancient pagan pre-Mohammed Arabian antiquity rock. In Morocco, especially, there is a complex latticework of Andalusian, Arabian, African, and classical Western rhythm.

Flamenco music of Spain is lifted directly from Morocco and the Moorish empire, and given a Spanish mustache.

The instruments which "help one to find the existence of the Truth behind the Veil":

  kanoun--a zither
  derbouka--a calabash tom-tom
  nwakess--castanets
  tar or duff--a tambourine
  kamanja--a sort-of violin
  oud--a turtle-shell lute

The rise of the dervish and Sufi teachings in Morocco in the 1200's cemented the political and spiritual future of music in this part of the Arab world. Before that, music seemed to suffer the same fate it does today: it related to the people, but Agnew and the FCC tried to lean on it. The popular kings and sultans always let music and art flourish at court--protected artists and thinkers of all kinds, in fact. Take a tip from the Fatimids, you future politicians--kick out the jams!

As they tell us in The Book of the Thousand Nights and a Night: "To some people music is meat, and to others medicine."

Scene: Marrakech. The middle of the night. A French-speaking Anglo couple decide to leave their blackbird garden for a short walk through the shadowed medieval arches of the medina.

Scarcely out of their gate they meet a Moroccan French teacher. He peppers them with questions and generally takes a shine to them. He lives in the same neighborhood, it turns out, and he invites them over to his place.

The MOROCCAN has a place behind a huge studded leather-covered arched door: a large inner court filled with tall palms and fountains, inward looking balconies and terraces, about eight rooms, and a rooftop view of the ancient walled city.

The three go into a small parlor. The MOROCCAN makes mint tea in a silver urn and they sit on thick red carpets, drink, and talk of Sufis. The MOROCCAN is interested in everything.

MOROCCAN (expressively): Je m'interesse en <u>tous</u>!

They talk of politics and revolution.

MOROCCAN (confidentially): I can speak freely with tourists, but with Moroccans--ah! You can't even trust your own brother! Anyway, it would be very difficult to change the government here. (He smiles sadly.)

They compare slang. In Arabic it's "tina" and "twenty." This only came out after great embarrassment to the MOROCCAN and persistent questioning by the Anglo GIRL. She wanted to know what the kids in the Jamaa el-F'na were <u>really</u> saying.
    After the <u>third</u> cup of tea and an exhausting Arabic lesson, the couple try to take their leave. They exchange names and addresses.

MOROCCAN: Ah, but I will accompany you and we will take a quick look at my little "maisonette."

They walk through a pitch-dark alleyway. The MOROCCAN takes the GIRL's hand and kisses it, to her confusion.
    The maisonette is small and simple. The MOROCCAN offers it to the Anglos should they ever return to Marrakech.
    It is the night of the full moon--the vernal equinox.
    As they descend the dark twisty stairs to the street, the GIRL somehow finds herself in between. Her husband is ahead, around a twist, and the MOROCCAN is just behind. He puts his hands on her shoulders and tries to turn her around to kiss her.

GIRL (confused and frightened): No! Don't!

She hurries downstairs to rejoin her husband, who knows nothing of the incident. At the foot of the stairs, the three join up again--the GIRL silent and seething, the husband pleasantly ignorant, and the MOROCCAN unusually talkative.

    As they walk back to the Anglos' garden, the GIRL clutching tightly to her husband's arm, the MOROCCAN breaks into song. He sings in the mode <u>melhoun</u>, a very ancient type of Moroccan music.

MOROCCAN: I am tremendously proud and happy
              To be visited by my Love:
              Zahra, the one with the beauty mark
              And the raised eyebrow;
              We have finally found each other again
              After our long separation--
              And we have gotten together
              In my automobile!

              And now we promenade together
              To the four corners of the world.

When the husband found out what had happened, he and his wife left town the next day. They have not returned since.

3   El-Loora el-Arbiya Wached el-Messela Deeal Notk: An Arabic Lesson

They've just sacked the library at Alexandria. Graduate students in Wisdom look up from their carrels, their highly developed intuitions and noses flashing them messages to HIT THE DIRT! One student, a cooler head than the rest, dashes for the locked cage where they keep the Old Commentary. He jimmies the lock, snatches up the precious and even now crumbly manuscript, and thrusts it under his robe. The knowledge must be preserved at all costs.

Behind the scenes the hidden symphony strikes up a new movement. Energy withdraws from Alexandria and regathers at Fez, in Morocco. About the year 1200 A.D. a group of adepts from all over the world meet in Fez to discuss the preservation of the Ancient Wisdom. They have had time to meditate on the meaning of the destruction of the greatest literary and scientific capital the world had yet known. As they confer, they realize they themselves symbolize the very problem they are trying to solve: the differences in language and philosophical terminology prevent a clear rendering of the Ancient Wisdom common to all.

The wise men at this point retire to their native countries, pledging to think over the problem and meet again in a few months' time.

Time passes and they meet again. Someone (perhaps a Chinese magician?) suggests the idea that they reduce the Ancient Wisdom to a series of pictures. Another adept (a Hebrew?) recommends basing the new expression of the Ageless Wisdom on the harmonies of numbers. A third (no doubt an Arab) advocates disguising the entire thing as a deck of playing cards, so as to circumvent future book burnings.

Thus we witness the birth of the Tarot.

Do you love your language? Would you fight a jihad--
a holy war--for it? Ponder the Arabs, who conquered the
world from Morocco to Malaya and insisted upon nothing
but the adoption of the Arabic language. Conversion to
Islam followed like a camel follows a block of burning
hashish.

Psychologists today are getting around to the fact
that one's language might have something to do with the
way one understands. Mastering Arabic means mastering a
whole cosmology.

Cut the tapes stereoed into your intellect;
Dedicate a new bridge
For swimmers only.

Spiriting away the prison bars--
Keeping the faith while cleaning
   the jailhouse johns.

Eyes open wide as wild geese;
Mysterious notation--
        Sluice right past the censor,
        Whose vision is blinded
        By its astonishing clarity.

Il faut mordre des idées afin des bien accueillir.

Journal entry, Tuesday, May 5 (yoom el-tleta):

    Arab lingo all mumbo-jumbo.
    Any bright light can pick it up--
    But you never know where it's been!

    Ten forms capable
    Of infinite ciphertext expansion.

    The trick in French is to speak with the lips; in Arabic, you speak with the heart. To fully comprehend Arabic one might spell out verses from the Koran using the Tarot deck: each card corresponds to a letter of the alphabet. One might also encipher the Book into numbers (as we learned in the "Magic Lesson"): each card (and each letter) corresponds to a number. This same process, incidentally, works just as well with the Bible. Try spelling out the names of the Twelve Tribes in Tarot language.
    Learning the Arabic language is vital; that is to say, living. What to make of this Arab, this mirror image of ourselves? He writes from right to left, his eye is turned on the past, he leaves all to Allah. Do we dare know him?
    I say we must. Where else could we get such good hash?
    And how else could we understand our times here in old Armorica without understanding the culture, unconscious myth, and language which vivify our New Atlanteans? You know, the Wilhelm-Baynes translation of the I Ching is very good, excellent. But it was done in the last century. Words did not then exist in English or German to express some of the thoughts inherent in the ancient Chinese. The root-idea of "groovy," for instance, is predominant in the Chinese. I understand a new translation is underway.
    This language trip gets heavy when you consider how we ought to go about talking to beings we meet up with in outer space, or how we program Buckminster Fuller's World Game to register psychological facts. Mind you--the Arabic language

is not artificially constructed. It grew out of need and custom, like any other. But the harmonies of the alphabet with numbers were sensed and worked with from the outset. The same harmonies exist in all languages (in all life) whether we discover them or not. To put a Qabalistic system to language, be it Tarot or some kind of numerical substitution code, only reveals the <u>preexisting</u> harmonies in the universe. Only our consciousness evolves. In primitive form this manifests as the "languages" of our modern computers.

I leave it to computer heads to apply this. Here is the table of Arabic grammatical forms, with their general meanings:

Let "x x x" represent the typical three-letter Arabic root word.

1. ×× × = root word

2. ×ẍ× = idea of "doing" or "making"

3. ××|× = direct object

4. ×××| = meaning of the second, but more rapid

5. ×ẍ× ـتـ = reflexive of the second

6. ××|× ـتـ = reflexive of the third

7. ××× ـبـ اِ = reflexive or passive

8. ××× ـتـ ×اِ = reflexive or passive

9. ẍ××اِ = to become "x x x"

10. ××× ـتـسـاِ = to seek "x x x"

178

What we need are more simultaneous interpreters. Translate one caste into another. Align ears with the sound. Intuition works with mathematical precision and numerical accuracy. Man takes charge of his own evolution. This is the Aquarian Age, the Great Event, the Grand Opening Sail.

What we need are more geniuses. I mean two-fisted bisociators who understand many tongues. I mean generalists who aren't afraid to butt their heads against bloodstones. I mean light beacons who can open stuck pickle jars. What makes the Arab so deep a mystery is his uncanny ability.

The Arab doesn't need geniuses: he needs money.

So what did we get from the Arabs? What good is a summary when the book speaks for itself? We learned a new language and thus some new rules. We saw survival. We loosed myths from their moorings. We dealt ourselves into the all-at-once macro-micro nonsimultaneous card game, hustled hoopla, built model domes, dreamed of figure eights, saw great white horses on the misty mountainsides, stood on ancient ruins, learned the back country, listened to the drum, understood the ocean, manned the islands, found old friends. We renewed ourselves.

ALHAMDOLELIA!

ABOUT THE AUTHOR

David Saltman was born in Chicago in 1946. He spent the first four years of his life riding elevated trains, and the next eight playing in Pueblo ruins. He became a foreign correspondent at twenty--after graduating from the University of Michigan--and has traveled extensively throughout Europe, the Middle East, North Africa, Mexico, Canada, Asia, and the USA. He speaks nine languages fluently, is an expert magician, an experienced gardener and backwoodsman, and a student of everything out of the ordinary. He has flown kites at Stonehenge, is deadly accurate with the boomerang, and knows his mushrooms.
    He has written for The New York Times, The National Observer, National Educational Television, CBS Radio Group, ABC News, UPI Audio, the Canadian Broadcasting Corporation, and various other print and broadcast media.
    He is happily married to Barbara, a painter and sculptor. Since leaving Morocco and England, they have lived on a remote farm in the Adirondack Mountains, in a Spanish house in the middle of Los Angeles, and across from a Buddhist temple in Kuala Lumpur.